ADMINISTRATOR'S
HANDBOOK
★ ★ ★ ★ ★ for ★ ★ ★ ★ ★
IMPROVING
FACULTY
MORALE

by

Loyd D. Andrew, David J. Parks,
Lynda A. Nelson, and the Phi Delta Kappa
Commission on Teacher/Faculty Morale

Phi Delta Kappa
Bloomington, Indiana

Cover design by Charmaine Dapena

The Phi Delta Kappa Commission on Teacher/Faculty Morale

Loyd D. Andrew
Virginia Polytechnic Institute

Juliana Boudreaux
New Orleans Public Schools

Richard Ebert
Cholla Elementary School
Phoenix, Arizona

Scott Geller
Virginia Polytechnic Institute

Michael Marcase
Philadelphia Public Schools

Lawrence McCluskey
Virginia Polytechnic Institute

Lynda A. Nelson
Virginia Polytechnic Institute

David J. Parks
Virginia Polytechnic Institute

James Sandfort
Shawnee Mission East High School
Shawnee Mission, Kansas

Keith Zook
Computer Systems
Grosse Ile, Michigan

Case Study Researchers

Fred Fifer
University of Texas at Dallas

George D. Gates
Idaho State University

Betty Lapido
Northwestern University

Richard L. Sagness
Idaho State University

Barbara Schneider
Northwestern University

Acknowledgments

Many helped in this study. The Commission members contributed greatly by identifying the administrative practices associated with morale that were the focus of the study. They also assisted in obtaining nominations of schools with good and poor morale. A particular debt of gratitude is owed to the schools and their staffs who completed surveys and allowed themselves to be studied.

However, the greatest appreciation is owed to Barbara Schneider and Betty Lapido at Northwestern University, Richard Sagness and George Gates at Idaho State University, and Fred Fifer at the University of Texas at Dallas. They conducted six of the 10 case studies. They spent hours interviewing board members, administrators, and teachers. They sifted through hundreds of sheets of data to prepare reports from which this handbook was developed. Without their help this handbook could not have been written.

The authors also greatly appreciate the financial support of Phi Delta Kappa International to carry out this study. Derek L. Burleson, editor of special publications, provided criticism and advice that was badly needed. We also are indebted to Paulette Gardner, who typed many drafts rapidly and well and with better humor than we deserved. There are others who made this work possible: those who nominated school districts for participation, librarians, graduate students, and administrators.

None of the above, of course, are responsible for any errors and omissions. The authors take full responsibility for those that may exist.

Table of Contents

Preface

Teacher morale in the United States is probably the lowest it has been in 40 years. The National Commission on Excellence in Education (1983) expressed concern about the "rising tide of mediocrity" in education; the College Board (1983) associated the decline in Scholastic Aptitude Test scores to lowered academic standards; the Twentieth Century Fund Task Force on Federal Elementary and Secondary Education Policy (1983) contended that the schools are in danger of losing sight of their fundamental purpose. The Gallup Poll of Public Attitudes Toward the Public Schools (Gallup 1983) reported that only 45% (down from 75% in 1969) of the respondents would want a child of theirs to take up teaching as a career and that only 19% of the respondents rated the public schools in the nation either an A (2%) or a B (17%).

These statistics alone should be enough to create low morale among teachers. But there are other conditions that have contributed to the decline in teacher morale. Compensation and benefits for teachers have not kept pace with those in comparable fields of work; the clientele in classrooms has changed radically; values of our society are in transition; and economic conditions do not bode well for education.

The major recommendation to date for improving economic incentives has been to offer merit increases to a few. A few governors, legislators, and taxpayers have recognized publicly that times have changed and that competitive pay must be offered to attract the best and brightest to education. Women, who now enjoy more career options, will no longer accept the low pay typically found in teaching.

Of course, teacher salaries are not the only source of difficulty. There have been radical changes in society. Since 1960 the number of single-parent families has increased greatly. Divorce has become commonplace. There are an increasing number of two-career families. Schools have been asked to do more. In fact, they have increased their problems by *being successful* in providing more and longer educational opportunities. In 1960 only 65.1% of 17-year-olds were high school graduates; in 1980, 73.6% of this group had graduated from high school. In 1960 only 60.7% of the population, 25 or older, had completed four years of high school or more; the percentage of blacks and other races was 21.7%. By 1980 these percentages were 85.8% and 77.1%, respectively.

The clientele of school systems now includes those formerly excluded by race or handicap. Children with psychological, physical, and emotional handicaps are no longer turned away. Because our schools have tried to do more, there have been more failures, including discipline problems, just as there have been more successes.

Phi Delta Kappa has been in the forefront in addressing many of the problems facing our schools today through its publications, programs, and projects. It has funded several commissions to carry out studies of these problems. One of these was the Commission on Teacher/Faculty Morale, whose mission was to determine what might be done by administrators to improve teacher/faculty morale.

The Commission worked on the study of administrative practices as they affect teacher morale for more than three years. Its membership included university faculty, elementary and secondary teachers, elementary and secondary principals, and superintendents.

In carrying out its work, the Commission: 1) reviewed recent research and theory on morale, 2) conducted a two-phase study to assess the current status of teacher morale and to verify some of the relationships among variables found in the review of the literature (phase one was a national survey, phase two was 10 case studies of schools with good and poor morale), and 3) prepared this handbook. We invite you to consider the results of our efforts.

Loyd D. Andrew
David J. Parks
Lynda A. Nelson

1

Introduction and Overview

As in the past, our schools again are being blamed for much of what is wrong in the United States. The President's National Commission on Excellence in Education (1983) described our schools as a "rising tide of mediocrity" in *A Nation at Risk*. The proportion of parents who would like their children to become public school teachers has declined from 75% in 1969 to 45% in 1983 (Gallup 1983). These indictments alone should be enough tc damage the morale of teachers, administrators, and even students. Yet morale and academic achievement in some schools are high, in others low, according to our own and other studies. This would suggest that national perceptions of the teaching profession and of education as a whole do not dampen the spirits of all and that local rather than national factors affect morale. It was the premise of Phi Delta Kappa in 1982 that one of those factors might be administrative behavior. For this reason, Phi Delta Kappa commissioned a study to determine what administrative practices, if any, had an effect on the morale of teachers.

Why Study Morale?

Morale is closely linked to organizational survival and to productivity; it is more than something "nice to have." If the challenges of *A Nation at Risk* are to be met, positive steps must be taken to improve the morale of teachers, students, and administrators in those school systems that have low morale, which are likely to be in the preponderance at the moment.

Much has been written about morale. Many instruments have been designed to assess the morale of individuals or groups in different types of organizations. There is some sound as well as considerable shallow research on morale and those factors that affect it. Yet it is difficult to identify a paradigm

1

that fully describes those human and organizational factors that influence morale; it is even more difficult to find a paradigm that links the morale of staff to specific administrative practices.

In *The Motivation to Work* (1959) Herzberg complains about the human relations approach to management, which advocates practices to make employees "feel good" about themselves and their organization. He observes that advocates of this school of management were never able to show a link between feeling good and productivity. But morale is more than feeling good about oneself or one's organization. Indeed, one of the problems in studying factors affecting morale and in developing a handbook on good administrative practices for improving morale is that some of the practices proposed are not those given first priority by those trying to improve the economic and working conditions of employees in school systems. Working conditions and economic benefits are important and deserve much attention. The problem with many of the recent reports on the condition of education is that they focus on what is wrong with our schools without making many strong recommendations for providing necessary resources for improving working conditions and improving effectiveness. Administrative practices affecting morale are definitely linked to working conditions, organizational climate, and such productivity measures as student achievement.

Purposes of the Study

The Phi Delta Kappa Commission on Teacher/Faculty Morale was established to do the following:

1. Identify internal and external characteristics of school systems that are successful in achieving or maintaining high morale;
2. Identify instruments useful for evaluating teacher/faculty morale; and
3. Produce a handbook of promising practices for improving teacher/faculty morale.

After reviewing approximately 300 reports on morale and most of the psychological, sociological, and administrative/management literature related to morale, organization, and motivation (not all of which are listed in the references), the Commission surveyed 315 schools to determine their morale and conducted case studies in 10 schools to determine what factors affected morale.

The study deliberately concentrated on administrative practices; however, in choosing the schools for case studies an attempt was made to control for other factors that might affect morale, for example, socioeconomic level of the community, teacher salary levels, and state governance systems. The study team believes that it controlled for these factors in its design reasonably well but recognizes the serious limitation of the small sample of case studies. The small sample limited the amount of information that could be obtained on such factors as administrative personality and management style; local politics; and the values, attitudes, and practices of school boards, which often constrain administrative practice.

However, the Commission believes that what it recommends as good administrative practice is well grounded in theory and in the research of this study and other studies. The practices will work when values and behavior are congruent and when the political climate and attitudes of the school board are right.

Methodology of the Study

The Commission's first task was to review the literature to determine what theory and research had to offer concerning the relationship of administrative practice to morale.

The second task was to develop survey instruments for assessing morale in school systems and protocols for conducting case studies in a selected number of schools.

The third task was to conduct surveys to determine which schools had good and poor morale. This was done in two ways. First, representatives of state departments of education and state teacher organizations were asked to identify some schools with good and poor morale. Second, 315 schools, drawn at random, were surveyed.

The fourth task was to conduct case studies at selected schools. Four experienced investigators conducted these studies in Texas, Illinois, Idaho, Arkansas, and Tennessee. Two school systems were used in each state, one with reportedly good morale, the other with reportedly poor morale. Schools in Arkansas and Tennessee were used for pilot testing the case-study protocols. The schools were located in urban, suburban, and rural environments and were matched as closely as possible for socioeconomic and political conditions.

The case-study investigators were not informed beforehand about the perceived morale of the schools. However, their assessments of morale corresponded to the assessments obtained from the representatives of education departments and teacher organizations. The investigators interviewed superintendents, associate superintendents, principals, teachers, and students at the schools used in the case studies. In addition, at the schools in Texas, Illinois, Idaho, and Arkansas, the National Survey on Teacher Morale instrument was completed by approximately 10% of the teachers in the schools. The protocols and instruments used in the case studies are available for review at the authors' university.

The fifth task was to analyze the findings and to develop recommendations for good administrative practice, based on the literature that was reviewed and the research that was conducted.

Analysis. Two types of analysis were used in the study. Data from surveys and from instruments administered at the selected case-study sites were analyzed using descriptive statistics. These findings are reported herein only briefly because they did not provide much insight into administrative practices related to morale.

Data from interviews and observations were used to describe administrative practice at the selected schools. The interviews and observations were designed to be open-ended and exploratory; however, some focus (and thus some bias) was provided for the study by propositions developed from the theory and research synthesized from the review of the literature. These propositions are discussed in Chapter 2. It is unlikely that this focus overly biased the findings, since four different teams of investigators were used, and each had the freedom to explore beyond the protocols. In addition, the findings in several instances went beyond what had been hypothesized.

What We Have Done

We have ascertained with fair reliability that administrative practice does make a difference. We also have synthesized much of the theory on educational administration that appears to pertain to improving morale (much more needs to be done) and have outlined a partial path through the ambiguity of the literature. We have made suggestions for administrative action to improve morale. An instrument has been designed to help practicing administrators assess their own behavior. We suggest some steps for changing behaviors when change is needed and provide a set of rules based on the case studies and literature.

Organization of the Handbook

Chapter 1 is a description of why and how the study was conducted.

Chapter 2 contains what was learned from the literature. It is that and a bit more. An attempt has been made to provide a synthesis of several theories on administration as these relate to practice in schools with good morale and relatively good productivity. Perhaps the major contribution from this synthesis is the recognition that schools are part of a community system and that administrators have to operate within the constraints of the community, as well as within constraints imposed by previous practice in the school. That administrators can do this and be effective if they practice some of the recommendations set forth in this handbook is supported by the case studies and other research.

Chapter 3 is a description of schools with good morale contrasted with the characteristics of schools with poor morale.

Chapter 4 is an action plan for the administrator. It discusses the relationship between morale and leadership, interpersonal relationships, rewards, workload, control mechanisms, professional development opportunities, and extra-school factors. Specific guidance is given.

Chapter 5 provides an instrument for diagnosing a leader's strengths and weaknesses so that he or she can determine which suggestions in Chapter 4 should be given priority in a particular plan for improving morale.

Chapter 6 contains 12 brief rules for administrators.

The references, while not exhaustive, include those books and articles that were found most helpful in synthesizing the theory, designing the research protocols and instruments, and analyzing the results of the research. The Appendix is a score sheet for leaders to assess their potential for improving morale.

2

Morale and Administration:
A Review of Theory and Research

The importance of morale on the health and effectiveness of an organization is suggested by the quantity of literature on the subject. Unfortunately, much of what has been written about morale does not consider its relationship to productivity and to administrative practice. In this chapter we have attempted to tie together what has been developed by other researchers on morale, productivity, and administrative theory in order to: 1) provide the background for understanding the propositions that were tested during the study, 2) enable the reader to evaluate the findings of this study against previous findings and theory development, and 3) provide a handy synthesis of the literature.

Concern with the relationship of morale to organization and leadership is not limited to school systems. Authors in the fields of sociology, psychology, business management, and educational administration are approaching, but have not yet arrived, at a single theory of administrative style for enhancing morale and organizational effectiveness.

It has been said that one criterion for being a good manager is the ability to handle ambiguity. Trying to make sense out of the literature on administration strongly tests this ability. For example, there is a body of literature and research that extols the benefits to workers and organizations if administrators would provide an environment that gives workers an opportunity to participate in decision making, considerable autonomy in defining tasks, and considerable freedom to self-actualize. Then there is a body of literature that concentrates on discipline, work standards, and use of salary as the major motivator for performance. This latter body sometimes appears less axiological and more practical than the first because it is often supported by experience in the field. However, it may be no more useful in reality than the first. In fact, what appear to be contradictions between the two bodies of work are often artifacts of the writers' or readers' perspectives. It is hoped that this synthesis of the literature will reduce the ambiguity by providing a neutral perspective.

Defining Morale

Writings on the subject of morale are ambiguous. There is considerable confusion about what it is, how it should be measured, and whether it is a useful concept in terms of productivity.

Webster's New World Dictionary provides a useful definition for purposes of identifying those administrative practices that can improve morale. Morale is defined as the "moral or mental condition with respect to courage, discipline, confidence, enthusiasm, willingness to endure hardship, etc., within a group, in relation to a group, or within an individual." The definition emphasizes the multi-dimensionality of the concept. It also includes the idea of "willingness to endure hardship." While this idea is not foreign to many school administrators and teachers, it is generally not included in the literature on morale, except from authors writing on military morale and leadership, who recognize that this "willingness" is one, if not the major, criterion for assessing morale.

Credence is given in the research to multi-dimensionality, though many authors tend to emphasize one dimension to the exclusion of the others. For example, Bentley and Rempel (1980) and Smith (1966) offer definitions of morale that emphasize the individual's state of mind. Bentley and Rempel, authors of a widely used instrument for measuring morale, define it as "the professional interest and enthusiasm that a person displays towards the achievement of individual and group goals in a given job situation" (p. 2). Smith, after analysis of colloquial use, definitions of experts, and its historical roots, defines morale as "a forward-looking and confident state of mind relevant to a shared and vital purpose" (p. 145).

Shared Purpose

The idea of shared purpose may be over-emphasized in definitions of morale. There are other important components, such as sense of belonging, challenge, shared excitement, and shared danger or discomfort, that rarely are embodied in definitions of morale. For example, Viteles (1953) defines morale as "an attitude of satisfaction with, desire to continue and willingness to strive for the goals of a particular group or organization" (p. 12).

This emphasis on shared group purposes tends to inhibit understanding of morale from an administrator's point of view because it overlooks the influence of individual personalities on morale. Definitions such as Viteles' would seem to suggest that the greater the subordination of individual needs and goals to the group, the better the morale of the organization. This is not necessarily so. Indeed, such subordination is probably not healthy for either the individual or the organization in the long run.

The dangers of such subordination of self are described by Whyte, writing in the Fifties, and Maccoby, writing in the Seventies. Subordination of individual goals and needs to organizational purposes generally leads to depression or, to use the current term, "burnout." Whyte (1956) identified these candidates for burnout as "the ones . . . who have left home, spiritually as well as physically, to take the vows of organization life" (p. 3). Maccoby (1976) observed that company men "equate their personal interest with the corporation's long term development and success . . . but their belief in the company may transcend self-interest" (p. 89).

According to Maccoby, the typical company man tends to resist change and to subject his wishes and desires to help others. Self-descriptions give an impression of "constant self-comparison, self-monitoring, self-criticism, and analysis of interpersonal situations." Hector Rose in C.P. Snow's novels of English society is one of these company men. He is routinely gracious, almost excessively polite, loyal to his master (whatever the party), but even more so to the organization. Rose sacrificed personal relationships on and off the job to career and organizational requirements. Eliot Lewis, who worked with Rose for 20 years, was never invited to Rose's home to meet his wife. They knew each other only in the context of their organizational life. Rose had little room for self-development beyond what was necessary to get ahead and to meet the goals of the organization as he understood them. One of the more successful company men interviewed by Maccoby, one who had sacrificed his personal goals and needs to the company, had poor morale manifested in "depression, anxiety, restlessness, obsessive doubt, back troubles, and finally serious gastrointestinal difficulties." A less successful company man felt that he had "sold himself to the devil" and described himself as a "hollow man," one who was afraid he felt "nothing" (p. 95).

A school system with many teachers of this type is not likely to have either good morale or effective teaching. Those who subordinate their goals to organizational goals would appear, from Whyte's and Maccoby's studies, to be those who have difficulty in relating sincerely and intimately with others. They resist change, are excessively anxious, and lack a sense of play.

A second type of personality found by Maccoby in many organizations was the "craftsman." This type does not easily subordinate personal goals to those of the organization. Maccoby has described this person as the "traditional builder, farmer, artisan. . . . More than any other character type he has a sense of limits — of materials, energy, knowledge, and the moral constraints — that must be respected to live a good life" (p. 31). Like the best teachers or the best of workers in the field, they have a strong sense of self-worth, inventiveness, and a respect for the materials with which they work. The craftsmen that Maccoby studied differed from teachers in that they were object oriented rather than people oriented; they worked with materials of wood and steel and silicon, rather than with students. However, this difference may be superficial.

Maccoby found that craftsmen in corporations were invariably good fathers, fair disciplinarians, and easy to get along with. Respectful of authority, they had a sense of duty to do a good job for the organization. But problem solving, the nature of their work, and family were more important than organizational purpose. There is a sense in Maccoby's description that craftsmen do not think much about the organization and its purposes as long as it provides work that is challenging and a salary that enables them to be a good provider. When their organization did not provide challenging work, he found that they were likely to seek moonlighting jobs that offered challenge, or they moved on.

It could be inferred from Maccoby that individual and organizational morale would be high in organizations with many craftsmen when the organization provides challenge and excitement. Organizational purpose and structure must meet the needs of the individuals. More important, achieving the purpose must provide challenge and excitement, an idea too often underemphasized in many definitions of morale.

Sense of Belonging

Underemphasized in many studies of morale is the idea of belonging. Mayo has stated that the urge to belong might be the strongest and most basic of human drives. "For all of us, feelings of security and certainty derive always from assured membership of a group" (cited by Whyte 1956, p. 39). Much of Japanese success in competing with the West has been attributed to the strong sense of membership or belonging the Japanese worker has with his company and fellow employees (see Pascale and Athos 1981 for one of many discussions about Japanese management style). Japanese employees and school systems benefit from a cultural indoctrination, reinforced by Japanese management style, that provides ready solutions to two of the problems that Talcott Parsons (1960) said organizations must solve: 1) integration — establishing and organizing a set of relations among the member units that serve to coordinate and unify them into a single entity; and 2) latency — the maintenance over time of the system's motivational and cultural patterns.

Solving these problems often conflicts, of course, with solving Parsons' two other problems for social systems: 1) adapting to changing external conditions, and 2) defining objectives and obtaining resources for meeting those objectives. Discussion of such conflict is common in the literature on administration. Practical administration often requires balancing gains and losses when striving to optimize among objectives. Trying to provide an environment that optimally provides for all of Parsons' organizational problems is one of the challenges of administration.

9

In today's climate it is not easy for the administrator to create a sense of belonging. Some observers of Japanese management suspect that the Japanese will have increasing difficulty in maintaining group cohesiveness as their society grows in affluence and workers begin to question traditional values, one of the conditions that appears necessary if inventiveness is to be encouraged. Mayo (1960) saw the loss of belongingness or "social cooperation" as a major fault of industrial society. Social alienation reached such an extent in the 1970s that many social psychologists have labeled the decade as narcissistic. Freudenberger (1980) has asked, "In a society where we have killed our gods, exorcised our ghosts, separated from our parents, and left our neighborhoods behind . . . against what restraints do we forge our standards?" (p. 5). The craftsmen would probably answer, against your own. Herzberg would argue that work establishes its own standards, that free workers find satisfaction in work itself, and that much of the problem with school systems, as with most assembly-line organizations, is that specialization has robbed craftsmen of ownership in their work.

F. Tannenbaum (1951), like Mayo, has decried the loss of a sense of belonging in the industrial age; but he thought the unions might fill the social void that modern industrialization created. Teacher unions may be filling this role, particularly during periods of stress. Tannenbaum observed that trade unions "become an all-embracing way of life."

A.S. Tannenbaum is critical of the use of human relations techniques for providing a sense of belonging. In *Hierarchy in Organizations* (1974), a comparative cross-cultural study, he expressed concern about the manipulative nature of human relations techniques, particularly those that purportedly fostered participation in decision making. Tannenbaum and his collaborators found that American, Austrian, and Italian organizations were not as participative in decision making as were Israeli kibbutzim or Yugoslavian plants. At the same time, they found that American workers, though "they are powerless with respect to basic policy issues," did not feel as alienated as Italian workers. To quote Tannenbaum, "Italian workers know they are without power and quite realistically, they feel alienated. . . . American workers, on the other hand, appear well adjusted and they report high levels of opportunity and satisfaction. *Some actually feel a sense of responsibility in their plant — at least more than do workers in other places.* [Italics added] But this is only because the 'human relations' approach is so effective in its manipulation" (Tannenbaum et al. 1974, p. 220).

Clark Kerr, chancellor of the University of California System, expressed these concerns as early as the 1950s:

> The danger is not that loyalties are divided today but that they may be undivided tomorrow. . . . I would urge each individual to avoid total involvement in any organization; to seek to whatever extent lies within his power to limit each group to the minimum control necessary for performance of essential functions. (1953)

10

It may be that some of the social turmoil of the Sixties and the alienation of the Seventies was in reaction to the suffocating organizational loyalty that was fostered in the Fifties. According to Freudenberger, prime candidates for burnout are those who are overcommitted and overdedicated to some organizational goal when the goal has been externally imposed. Herzberg has observed that teachers and others in the helping professions are often asked to sublimate their needs to meet the socially imposed goals of being helpful and self-sacrificing. Thus, management must tread carefully when creating a sense of "organizational belongingness."

For organizations to be effective, the members must have ownership in the purpose of the organization; values must be shared. While there must be a sense of belonging, manipulation to obtain that sense of belonging can lead to poor morale and other dysfunctions, not least of which is for employees to fail to be spontaneous and innovative in their contributions. Company men and bureaucrats, even during their most productive years with an organization, generally fail in providing spontaneous and innovative ideas, a critical behavior for institutional adaptability. As Katz and Kahn (1966) have observed, leaders must provide an organization that attracts and keeps members who 1) meet the requirements of their position and 2) are spontaneous and innovative.

Administrative Theory and Morale

Peters and Waterman in *In Search of Excellence* (1982), their study of America's best-run companies, found that these companies have an organizational structure, management style, and service philosophy that boosts employee pride and morale. They report that "excellent companies" give employees responsibility, praise, and respect. Their findings suggest that high organizational and individual morale in these companies is attained by reducing or countering the stress factors that Mayo complained about a quarter of a century ago and that Cedoline (1982) contends are often responsible for burnout, though he recognizes that a person's ability "to cope varies not only with environment . . . and social conditions, but also with heredity, training and health" (p. 3).

Low morale is associated with frustration, alienation, and powerlessness. Belongingness, togetherness, achievement, and self or group esteem are generally associated with high morale. This section reviews the literature on those practices school administrators might use to reduce alienation and to create a sense of belongingness, togetherness, achievement, and self and group esteem.

The literature on administrative theory contains several ideas that appear to be contradictory. The first contradiction is between the concept of authority and the concept of staff involvement in decision making. Earlier mention was made of A.S. Tannenbaum's finding that there was less alienation when

11

workers believed that they were active participants in the decision-making process, whether or not this was true. In contrast, Barnard (1966) is a strong advocate of authority, seeing the establishment and maintenance of authority as essential for organizational effectiveness. At the same time, he would appear to be an advocate of some staff participation in the governance of an organization.

Another contradiction in the literature is the conflict between the staff "buying into" the mission and goals and values of the organization and the danger of this "buy in" to personal morale when it is externally imposed.

A third contradiction concerns what Herzberg (1976) has labeled hygiene factors, involving such working conditions as office furnishings and amount of red tape, as well as salary. His and others' research would appear to support his thesis that these factors, at best, do little to improve either morale or motivation, though they often contribute to worker dissatisfaction. However, his thesis is contradicted by research that suggests that material rewards do motivate employees. For example, salesmen are often motivated by commissions, company presidents are motivated by the prospect of large bonuses, and merit pay plans are now being recommended as a way to educational "excellence." When merit pay was instituted in the federal civil service during the late Seventies, the outcomes were mixed. Such plans are sometimes useful for recruiting or holding "good" people; whether they change other behaviors is less clear.

A fourth conundrum for those seeking guidance for administrative practice is closely related to the third. Despite the findings of Mayo and of later researchers that working conditions have little effect on morale or productivity or sense of belonging, there are strong advocates of such solutions to improving morale and productivity. Moreover, there is a tendency in companies to initiate practices that make it easy for employees to feel part of the organization, although research (see Aronson 1984) and regular observation of groups with high morale would suggest that feelings of belonging, group loyalty, and group pride are often in direct proportion to the costs required for acceptance into membership. Initiation rites of fraternities and sororities and hazing in military schools may be dangerous and appear somewhat silly to outsiders, but they seem to be effective for instilling loyalty in members of the group. Similarly, those advocating increasing the dues for becoming a member of the teaching profession by imposing an additional round of competency tests beyond those given in colleges of education have some precedents to support their cause.

A fifth contradiction in administrative practice involves varying theories for modifying behavior. Psychology offers several theories, but no recipes, for changing behavior. There are behavioral, cognitive, and psychoanalytical theoretical models. Advocates of each model have substantive research to support their methods for changing behaviors and values, but there has been little integration of the different approaches at the theoretical level, although many clinicians use a combination and label their approach eclectic. An eclectic approach, or what some authorities call situational management, uses each of the above theories as circumstances dictate and resources allow. It is probably the best way for practicing administrators to achieve the multiple objectives of those who make up a school system — administrators, classified staff, teachers, parents, students, and several special interest groups.

Some guidance for successful practice of administrative eclecticism is provided by Thompson's propositions (1967) concerning which leadership style operates best under given situations. Thompson has observed that in some organizations there is high agreement among the members of the organization on mission and goals; in others, like school systems, there is much less agreement among members and constituencies about objectives.

There also are some operations that lend themselves to precise definition of objectives and to a best way of accomplishing a task. Such operations are found in industries like steel, textiles, and other assembly-line industries where Taylor (1914) and his followers conducted time and motion studies in order to determine the most efficient procedures for performing tasks. In those organizations where there is strong agreement on objectives and procedures for accomplishing the objectives, there does not appear to be much need, either operationally or psychologically, for members of the organization to spend much time discussing what is to be done and how it should be done. The success of the industrial era in the U.S. was due to authoritative management, supported by the inventiveness of relatively few scientists and engineers, since everyone was in agreement on what the goals were and what operations were best suited for attaining those goals. It was possible and still is possible and beneficial to simplify management by defining tasks very precisely. Eli Whitney demonstrated the practicality of specialization, and Henry Ford and many others applied it in assembly-line production.

However, precise goals and means to achieve them do not apply in teaching and other helping professions; nor do they apply in high tech industries, where most of Peters and Waterman's "excellent companies" were found. In school systems, there is considerable debate about objectives. And there is as much disagreement in schools about the best way of achieving some objectives (for example, teaching reading) as there is in high tech industry on designing adaptive intelligence machines.

This would suggest that administrators of school systems would do well to involve those who will be charged with carrying out decisions in the process of defining the goals. However, such administration requires practicing some fundamental principles.

The first principle is the Katz and Kahn (1966) dictum: For an organization to be effective, the administrator must provide an organizational environment that 1) is attractive to those who can meet the requirements of their position in the organization, and 2) encourages innovative and spontaneous activities and ideas. The second item may be irrelevant in those organizations where the way to perform tasks has been tightly specified. In those organizations, robots are now performing some of the tasks. But school systems are not that type of organization; they require exceptional innovation and spontaneity.

Three other principles, articulated by Barnard (1966), are:

1. It is important to establish and maintain authority.
2. Members of organizations have zones of indifference. There are certain orders and directions to which members of organizations are indifferent. They will accept them without questioning. There are others — those that affect their value or needs systems — that they will not accept with indifference.
3. Communication of decisions and directions should be formally authenticated.

Two of Barnard's rules for effective organizational functioning are: 1) the line of communication should not be interrupted during the time when the organization is to function, and 2) every communication should be authenticated. The first rule demands that offices be temporarily filled when the regular officer is absent or ill. If this does not occur, according to Barnard, both the formal and informal organizations will break down. He observed that "if the position is left empty, but the fact were not known, an organization might function for a considerable time without serious disturbance, except in an emergency. But if known, it would quickly become disorganized." For authenticating the communication links, he observed that the filling of positions should be "dramatized, an essential process to the creation of authority at the bottom, . . . It is, essential to 'organization loyalty and solidarity' " (p. 180).

Barnard's advice on decision making is that "the fine art of executive decision consists in not deciding questions that are not now pertinent, in not deciding prematurely, in not making decisions that cannot be made effective, and in not making decisions that others should make" (p. 194).

Barnard's advice is supported in the works of Simon (1976) and Griffiths (1959), who believed that the essential element of administration is the regulation of the decision-making process. Griffiths observed that the specific function of administration is to develop and regulate the decision-making process in the most effective manner possible. It is sometimes assumed that the function of the chief executive officer is to make the decisions because others are incompetent to do so. Griffiths argues that the "function of the executive [for example, the superintendent, principal, or supervisor] is to see to it that the decision process proceeds in an effective manner" (p. 172).

For our purposes here the question is: How should authority, communication, and the decision-making process be established in school systems to enhance a sense of belongingness, to reduce alienation, to increase self and organizational esteem, and to reduce frustration resulting from a sense of powerlessness? The three — authority, communication, and the decision-making process — are intertwined.

Authority

Authority, the first prerequisite for effective organization, is well established (at least at a theoretical level) in the school system. There is generally a set of rules or policy that defines relations among the school board, administrators, teachers, classified employees, and students. However, this authority can be diluted by: 1) the informal and sometimes illegitimate influence of school board members, parents, or community leaders; 2) contradictions among laws and regulations; and 3) varying perspectives on the mission of the schools. The conflict is illustrated in a letter to the editor of a paper in a small school district in North Carolina:

> The schools, as educational institutions, are charged by our society to bring our children to a level of social competence that enables them to function productively in life. The simple fact is that a school must be responsive to the desires of a local community and to its needs. These two are not the same. The needs of a community are seen in preparing students for further academic work and for places in the productive life of this nation. There is no question that teachers must often make compromises with their own convictions in order to keep peace in a community. The closer teachers get to attempting to be totally responsive to the local desires the more they must compromise if they are themselves well educated (Stevenson 1982, p. 4).

Cuban (1976) reflected about conflicts over authority and the stress it puts on urban superintendents: "For most urban superintendents there was a perpetual crossfire of expectations, requests, and demands from board members, middle-level administrators, principals, teachers, students, and civic groups. . . . Much like a juggler [the superintendent] keeps a dozen objects in the air on a windy day . . . very uncertain whether he has the whole dozen but fearful of stopping to find out" (p. 26). Cuban believed that those superintendents in urban environments who maintained authority and survived in the Sixties and Seventies were "negotiator-statesmen." The concept "embraces the notion that either external or organizational conflict is inevitable, even basic to human affairs. Different interest groups are legitimate and somehow must be dealt with" (p. 29). The concept is a practical recognition of John Locke's argument that authority ultimately resides in the ruled. Locke was the first to observe that in a political sense people are ultimately sovereign. One quits one's "executive power . . . and resigns it to the public. . . . Freedom of men under government is to have a standing rule to live by . . . a liberty to follow his own will in all things . . . not to be subject to the inconstant, uncertain, unknown arbitrary will of another man."

Barnard (1966) recognized the same principles in operation in business and modern society, noting that he had observed even in Hitler's Germany "many violations of positive law or edict, some of them open and on a wide scale" (p. 162). He observed that "specific laws will be obeyed or disobeyed by the individual citizen" under certain "specific conditions." He noted that what is true for the larger society is also true for the small organization. "It is surprising how . . . in the best of organizations orders are disobeyed" (p. 162). Barnard was so concerned that executives might not accept Locke's principles as realistic that he quoted two different writers in support of his argument — a sociologist and a battlefield commander. Sociologist Roberto Michels has asserted that "Whether authority is of personal or institutional origin, it is created and maintained by public opinion, which in its turn is conditioned by sentiment, affection, reverence, or fatalism. Even when authority rests on mere physical coercion, it is *accepted* by those ruled, although the acceptance may be due to fear of force" (Quoted by Barnard, p. 164). Major General James G. Harbord observed that "the greatest of all democracies is an Army. Discipline and morale influence the inarticulate vote that is instantly taken by masses of men when the order comes to move forward — a variant of crowd psychology that inclines it to follow a leader, but the Army does not move forward until the motion has 'carried' " (Quoted by Barnard, p. 164).

One way to ensure that "the motion" will carry in complex organizations where there is not obvious agreement on objectives or means would be the employment of Likert's (1967) System Four type of management. In this system, leadership is highly participative and supportive; motivational and communication forces are strong; interaction is warm and close; decision making and goal setting are shared; and control processes are collegial as opposed to hierarchical. There is a strong emphasis on performance goals and training. According to research by Wagstaff (1969) and Cullens (1971), teachers and students are most satisfied in this type of school environment.

Hoy and Appleberry (1970) found that schools with "custodial, pupil-controlled orientation have significantly greater disengagement, less esprit and morale, more aloofness, and less thrust than those with a humanistic, pupil control orientation." Such schools are those in which two-way communication between pupils and teachers concerning discipline, learning goals, and performance is emphasized. In custodial schools a rigid pupil-teacher status hierarchy is maintained. There is little two-way communication, but much direction downward.

Communication

Despite the numerous texts written on the subject, techniques of effective communication need to be emphasized repeatedly. A successful communication will satisfy four conditions simultaneously:

First, what is wanted must be understood. Thus, there must be continuous feedback to ensure that what is said is heard and is correctly interpreted.

Second, what is wanted must be perceived by all parties as being consistent with the goals of the organization. This means that much effort must be spent on developing, discussing, and interpreting the goals of the organization.

Third, the communication must be clear in relationship to the needs and goals of the individual(s) who will be responsible for carrying out a decision or order. For members to be active participants in an organization they must feel, at both the cognitive and affective levels, that there is a fair contract between the organization and the member. Time must be devoted to discussing openly individual needs and resources.

Fourth, the individuals who accept the order or decision must not only be willing, as the result of one, two, or three above, to carry out the decisions but they *must be capable* of doing so. This means there must be serious assessment of skills and resources and probably continuous training — particularly if responsibilities and recognition are to be enhanced.

These conditions are so important to the authority of the administrator and organization that Barnard (1966) insists that "orders should not be issued that cannot or will not be obeyed . . . to do so destroys authority, discipline and morale" (p. 167). There are, of course, many ways for refusing orders and defying official authority. The most blatant is overt refusal or resignation. Generally, however, the disobedience is more subtle — systematic malingering, suboptimal performance, withdrawal, and sabotage. An organization experiencing these forms of disobedience can be characterized as having poor morale. Individuals displaying these characteristics may be victims of burnout and are not likely to have a sense of belonging to the school or to any group.

The literature suggests that the success and morale of the school will depend to a large extent on the administrator's ability to obtain a "grant of authority" from the students, parents, and other "customers" of the system. Communication is critical in obtaining this grant of authority, and administrators and their staffs must be sensitive to the concerns of these "customers." School leaders must communicate to those reporting to them that it is their responsibility to understand the value systems and needs of various constituencies and to communicate organizational goals and needs.

Communication is not telling people what to do, it is involving them in determining goals and needs and obtaining a consensus. Sergiovanni, Burlingame, Combs, and Thurston (1980) have offered the following advice for gaining a grant of authority from the constituency of the system. They make a distinction between educational administration — using the best means to achieve goals — and educational leadership — helping in the shaping of goals. Zaleznick (1977) has observed that leaders "are active instead of reactive, shaping ideas instead of responding to them. Leaders adopt a personal and active attitude towards goals. The influence a leader exerts in altering moods, evoking images and expectations, and in establishing specific desires and objectives determines the directions. . . . The net result . . . is to change the way people think about what is desirable, possible, and necessary."

Chandler and Petty (1955) give specific suggestions for providing educational leadership. After noting that the school should have an educational philosophy (a condition they apparently did not find too prevalent in 1955), they observed that teachers (particularly new ones) are faced with the "difficult problem of understanding, accepting, and contributing to the school's philosophy and objectives" (p. 161). They argue that the best method of getting such commitment is to involve teachers in the development of educational philosophy and policy. They offer the following suggestions: 1) establish the necessary framework, 2) define the extent of responsibility and authority of the group, 3) provide for voluntary participation, 4) select a program that is believed crucial by the group, 5) provide time for group work, 6) encourage emerging leadership, 7) demonstrate sincerity, and 8) devise a plan of evaluation.

Participatory management is not laissez-faire administration. Rather, the purpose of participatory management is to attain a willing grant of authority, using information, persuasion, and negotiation. Teachers, according to Chandler and Petty (1955), want to participate in policy formulation that affects "vocational preoccupation and interests" (p. 60). The leader who honestly assigns responsibility and authority for developing policy that will have an impact on diverse interests and biases must be willing and able to provide interpretative leadership, that is, help the group keep common objectives in view, keep the discussion on the main track, supply facts and ideas, and identify common ground as deliberation progresses (p. 61). "Unity of purpose is developed through cordial interpersonal relationships. Members of the staff must know and like each other because cooperation originates in feelings" (p. 61).

Feelings are obviously an important consideration in administration. Administrators who view people suspiciously and consider them lazy, dishonest, and irresponsible will not be able to gain a willing and cheerful acceptance of their authority. Rather, they will have to rely on coercion. Those who believe that people want to contribute and achieve can effectively use System Four management or a variation thereof, such as Miles' (1965) Human Resources Model. According to his research, when this management style is used, "faculty satisfaction will increase as a by-product of improved performance and the opportunity to contribute creatively to this improvement."

However, staff and community participation in making decisions about educational philosophy, mission, goals, and objectives is not likely to be enough to create high morale in a school system. Getting members of the system actively involved in deciding what ought to be done is an effective means for obtaining grants of authority and better decision making. However, organizational structure and job specification may thwart common human needs for growth and achievement. A great number of organizations, including many school systems, still suffer from some of the dysfunctions resulting from bureaucracy and the efficiency of scientific management, both of which advocate specialization and narrowly defined jobs as a means for achieving efficiency. However, gains in efficiency are often offset by losses in such areas as morale, cooperation, personal growth, and quality.

To counteract the negative features of bureaucratic management, Herzberg (1976) advocates what he calls vertical job loading or job enrichment. The key principles of vertical job loading are: 1) involvement of those who will participate in delivery of a product in planning the job, 2) immediate and direct feedback on doing the job, 3) assignment of responsibility, and 4) most important, job design that provides opportunity for "new learning, leading to unique expertise."

Vertical job enrichment has been tried in a few industrial plants. It seems to work well in research and development organizations and operates in conjunction with bureaucracies in the entertainment and media industries. The system generally involves the use of teams to accomplish a job as opposed to individuals doing a "bit of a job." Supervisors are eliminated as middlemen between the doers and the quality control inspectors. Errors are corrected by those who made them, not by another group or another worker. The virtue of this approach is individual growth and satisfaction from the work itself. Perhaps jobs in school systems should be redesigned using this approach.

However, neither Herzberg's motivation-hygiene theory nor his job enrichment programming is supported by all research studies. Sergiovanni (1967), in a replication of Herzberg's study in educational organizations, found that work itself and advancement were not significant as motivator factors. He reported that there are a lot of maintenance or routine tasks that are not exciting in themselves. Teachers also reported that there was little opportunity for advancement. From Sergiovanni's study one gets a picture of what Herzberg would describe as a typical assembly-line profile where some motivators — achievement and recognition — are increased and other motivators — work itself, responsibility, advancement, and growth — are depressed. He would argue that if these jobs were enriched, *the work itself* will become a motivator (Herzberg 1983). As Herzberg notes, evidence suggests that achievement and recognition "move only a minority of assembly line workers" (Herzberg 1976, p. 79).

Sergiovanni's findings that teachers do not find work itself and advancement to be motivators is contrary to what Herzberg and many other researchers have consistently found when the subjects were engineers, managers, and in some cases workers. Nor is Sergiovanni the only researcher to differ with Herzberg, particularly when the studies are conducted in educational settings. However, it may be that difference in findings is an artifact of the organizational systems where the research is conducted rather than some unique characteristics of teachers compared to other subjects. Teachers complain legitimately about little chance for advancement in their profession. In many school systems, there is not much job enrichment or team structure.

Of course, what Herzberg and Likert urge may not be an appropriate solution for all systems or for all workers. Dubin (1959) has observed that:

> work, for probably a majority of workers, and even extending into the
> ranks of management, may represent an institutional setting that is not
> the central life interest of the participants. The consequence of this is that
> while participating in work, a general attitude of apathy and indifference
> prevails. . . . Thus, the industrial worker does not feel imposed upon by
> the tyranny of organization, company, or union.

Strauss (1963) has serious reservations about imposing power-equalization (participatory) management in all cases. He has pointed out that "many individuals find relatively little satisfaction in their work, but this may not be as much of a deprivation as the hypothesis suggests, since many of these same individuals center their lives off the job and find most of their satisfaction in the community and home." While some are motivated by participation in organizational governance because it provides autonomy and self-actualization, there are "others whose greater needs are for security" and "who want to know what is expected of them." For them, "power equalization may . . . stir up a good deal of anxiety" (p. 267). They may be reluctant to accept the responsibility that participation imposes.

Strauss stressed the need to prepare people for participation. He also observed that "power-equalization techniques are not too meaningful when management needs no more than an adequate level of production, as is often the case when work is highly programmed" (p. 267). He questioned whether the gains in these cases would be worth the cost of redesigning jobs and supervisory techniques.

However, teaching is not a profession that lends itself to being highly programmed. There is ample evidence that school systems require innovative, spontaneous, and cooperative teachers to be effective, not teachers who, in Dubin's words, "while participating in work have a general attitude of apathy and indifference."

Strauss's and Dubin's counsel should not be dismissed out of hand when efforts are made to introduce participative management and job enrichment into an organization that has not previously had them. Some people are likely to be anxious about taking the responsibility that such management requires. They need to be prepared. The research suggests that gains from participative management and job enrichment (including team structure) is worth the cost of preparation and redesign of management systems when innovation is required.

Some of the Japanese success in competing with Western industry is attributed to their participatory management. In Japanese industry, the worker and his group are very much involved in determining how quality performance will be measured and enhanced. This involvement begins in the Japanese system of decision making, which, according to Drucker (1974), places emphasis not on finding an answer to a problem but on determining whether a decision is needed and on involving all of those who will be affected if a decision is made. In Japanese industry, the initial and most crucial step in decision making is in determining which group or groups should be involved in the process.

This involvement in the decision-making process extends from the executive level to the workers in the factory, who participate in quality circles where discussions and planning occur to improve processes. The Japanese concept is not entirely foreign to Western industry. IBM, one of Peters and Waterman's "excellent" companies, has practiced job enrichment for many years; and supervisors in its plants are identified as assistants. They are responsible for being sure that workers know their work and have the appropriate tools. At Hill Air Force Base, job enrichment involves having employees schedule their own work, maintain their vehicles, and do many inspections themselves. It has paid off in reduced costs, higher productivity, and better morale (Herzberg 1976, p. 173).

What can be derived from the above that may be related to ways of enhancing morale? In the following summary, some of the more critical ideas are synthesized as a prelude to stating propositions for testing in the 10 case studies conducted for this study of morale.

Summary

At the beginning of this chapter, it was observed that there is considerable ambiguity in both administrative theory and in the practice of administration concerning those factors that contribute to high and low morale. There are serious problems when trying to impose organizational goals and to create a sense of belonging at the same time. Yet effective organizations with high morale are those where the members believe in the mission of the organization and have a sense of belonging to the organization. Some schools of administration theory, particularly the human relations school, seem to imply that this sense of belonging can best be attained by making work pleasant, including making it easy to enter into membership in an organization. However, there is evidence that a sense of belonging is enhanced by the difficulty of entering a profession. We tend to value things, including membership, according to their cost. Not too much has been done in the literature of educational administration on how costs of membership in the teaching profession might increase the value of such membership and sense of belonging.

Considerable research has been done in education, as well as business administration, on how participation in decision making increases members' feelings of ownership of an organization's mission and goals. However, the value of such a management style is questioned by some writers. Some view it as a manipulative technique and doubt that power can or will be surrendered by administrators and the boards for whom they work. Others question it because they see the success of organizations depending on tough and authoritarian managers. Moreover, there is the example of organizations in the private and public sector that, when under stress, generally tighten hierarchical structures and increase reliance on salary increases and coercion as the primary motivators of their personnel. This is evident in the reaction of legislatures and school boards to the report of the Commission on Excellence in Education. Then there is the observation of Strauss and Dubin that all people are not ready for participation in governance and for the responsibility that it entails. There are those who simply want to work from 8 to 5 and to get their rewards outside the organization that pays their salary.

On the other hand, there is substantial research to demonstrate the value of involving members in mission and goal setting, particularly in those organizations where production cannot be highly programmed. Those organizations that involve the membership in decision making about objectives and that have flatter organizational structures tend to be distinguished by encouraging cooperation and contribution of innovative ideas.

Related research also strongly supports the argument that task specialization, as commonly practiced in most assembly-line industries and bureaucracies, creates dysfunctions because breaking down a job into small, routine tasks tends to deny the workers any ownership in the final product; any concern about quality; and the opportunity to grow, advance, and to enjoy the satisfaction of work well-done.

The more successful companies in the United States, like their Japanese competition, appear to be those that practice some form of participatory management and job enrichment, including team structures. In certain cases job enrichment is beginning to be used in industries that formerly used tight programming of work tasks and precise definitions of workers' responsibilities. Unfortunately, the literature in educational administration does not contain many examples of job redesign in school systems to provide for vertical job enrichment.

The contradictions in the literature and in practice may be that administrative theories have either been misinterpreted or not integrated. Certainly there is evidence that participatory management is viewed by some as surrender of authority. However, in good practice, authority is not surrendered. Participatory management recognizes that authority ultimately resides in the membership of an organization. Participatory management provides a means for attaining authority. It does not eliminate the need for the administrator to provide leadership and to participate in deciding on objectives. It does impose greater requirements to supply information and to persuade. It calls for clear communication and for putting in writing the policy, once it has been decided. It requires understanding that membership in an organization is generally broader than those over whom the administrator has direct authority. It requires the administrator to understand the values and needs of the members before persuading them to go in new directions. It must also be recognized that not all members of an organization want or have the skills to participate in mission setting and decision making. They must be prepared.

Propositions

A review of the literature on administrative theory led us to 13 propositions about administrative practices that will be prevalent in school systems with good teacher morale:

1. The authority of superintendents, principals, and teaching staff are well defined and publicly known. It is most likely that they are set forth in published policy and procedure manuals.
2. The school system is organized so that decisions are made at the lowest possible level, and training and consultation are available to ensure the success of delegated decision-making authority.
3. Administrators have authority and retain their responsibility for certain decisions, particularly in terms of recruitment, selection, and assignments.
4. The chief administrator and the staff have a fully developed and well-articulated educational philosophy.
5. Administrators provide leadership within and outside the formal school system in order to obtain consensus on philosophy and mission through some form of participatory management. At the same time, they minimize use of group processes for deciding on routine matters.
6. The school system is organized to facilitate both formal and informal communication among administrators, teachers, and board members.
7. Teachers are actively encouraged and supported in working with the community and in developing objectives that relate to community needs.
8. Administrators perceive themselves as being educational leaders and are active in shaping ideas and communicating philosophies, ideas, and values.
9. Administrators tend to view themselves as assistants to rather than supervisors of the teaching staff. That is, they see their job as one of enhancing and providing the support that teachers require for job satisfaction.
10. Administrators promote feelings of belongingness among the teaching staff, which is manifested by camaraderie among staff and between staff and administrators.
11. Teaching staff are relatively well paid in relationship to community standards. The administrators provide incentives and rewards to teachers through staff assignments, public recognition, and opportunities for professional development.
12. Administrators create a school environment that fosters feelings of self-respect among staff and students and promotes positive feelings toward the profession of teaching.
13. Administrators are concerned about opportunities for teachers to advance and grow. At the minimum, they provide strong staff development programs.

3

Administrative Practice
in Schools with Good Morale:
Findings from Case Studies

This chapter contains the conclusions of four teams of researchers who studied 10 school systems — two in urban environments, four in suburban areas, and four in rural districts. These research teams conducted their case studies using a rather simple interview protocol for investigating the 13 propositions identified in Chapter 2.

Although four different research teams studied schools in urban, suburban, and rural settings, their findings were consistent. The researchers did not know in advance the status of morale in the schools in their case studies; but almost from their first steps into a building, they sensed whether the school had high or low morale.

External conditions had some bearing on whether certain schools had good or poor morale. One of the school systems was recovering from the effects of a school board battle; another had recently suffered from a strike. In one of the rural systems, the majority of the teachers lived in a large city 30 miles away from their rural constituency. However, external conditions did not appear to be the major factor affecting a school's morale. More often the primary factor was administrative practice, particularly the administrator's ability to provide direction or leadership, internally and externally. Good morale was found in some schools and bad morale in other schools in the same district. In two cases morale had improved as a result of change in administration, in one instance a change in principal, in the other a change in superintendent.

Data were not found to test all the propositions associated with good morale. On the other hand, some of what was found was not anticipated. We hoped to find examples of job enrichment programs; we did not. But every school had fairly well-developed policy and procedure manuals; therefore, this characteristic did not distinguish one type of system from the other. Evidence also was insufficient to support the proposition that decisions in good morale schools are made at the lowest possible level and that training and consultation are available to ensure the success of delegated authority. However, one example was found of central office interference in making decisions that probably could have been made better at the building level. The interference had seriously upset the morale of the principal and his immediate staff. In another case, teachers complained about a long line-staff organization hampering communication with the principal. No direct evidence was discovered to support or refute the proposition that administrators in schools with good morale see themselves as assistants to rather than supervisors of teaching staff. In one school with poor morale, the principal described his role somewhat in those terms; but his other behaviors did not support such a role description.

More important than what was not discovered was what was learned that was not hypothesized, for example, the importance of personal characteristics of administrators.

Personal Characteristics of the Administrator

In the schools with better morale, principals were usually described as being outgoing, friendly, and good organizers. Such words as "open," "helpful," "student-centered," "systematic," "responsive," and "fair" were used. In schools with poor morale, principals were perceived as disciplinarians, inconsistent, nonsupportive, formal, and impatient. In no case where schools had been nominated as having poor morale did interviewees or researchers report that the administrator had open, warm, or consistent types of behaviors. One of the principals in a school with poor morale described his job as isolated and lonely, for "principals cannot share their stress with colleagues for fear of exposing their weaknesses."

One of the investigators asked teachers what they thought were desirable personal traits for a principal. The list of traits included the following: vitality and enthusiasm for the job, open and friendly, good listener, good authority figure, has an open-door policy, leads instead of pushes, flexible.

In a school with relatively poor morale, one team found that teachers viewed the principal as the "major influencing factor on morale." The teachers complained that a long line-staff organization often hampered communication between the teaching staff and principal. The principal was viewed by teachers as a professional but "alienated from his faculty." Teachers felt more at ease discussing problems with the assistant principal because of his accessibility and approachability.

Another team found many of the same administrator characteristics in the systems they studied. The teachers they interviewed described effective school leaders as ones who modeled democratic behavior, used team work, trusted teachers' judgements, were good listeners, were positive, often gave praise, and were assertive but not dictatorial. One individual was described as not being adequately assertive. He was characterized as "all talk and very little action."

In one school, a principal viewed the morale of his teaching staff as average or slightly below and gave himself a failing grade on morale. According to the researcher's report, "he attributed his low morale to his continuous contact with student discipline problems, long work days (65-70 hours per week), and dissatisfied teachers." This principal's opinion of students and teachers was in strong contrast to that of a superintendent in a high morale school located in a poor rural environment, despite the fact that teacher salaries were well below national norms (but good for the community) and buildings were badly in need of repair.

In the latter school district, neither the superintendent nor his high school principal worked 65-hour weeks, although they were rebuilding a system that had been disrupted only a year before with the removal of the previous superintendent. They were gradually introducing a new curriculum, some aspects of which would probably conflict with community values. The superintendent and the principal were optimistic about teachers and students. They showed strong respect for student rights as well as the rights of teachers. One of the innovations was the development of a student handbook and policy manual, regularly updated. The principal was new to administration; the superintendent was more experienced, having been successful in many administrative jobs of more complexity than the one he was currently filling. He delegated authority and responsibility and worked closely with community leaders and parents to involve them in helping the school set goals and obtain resources.

One research team commented on the importance of the administrator's positive attitude. They reported that in a good morale school the principal "maintained a healthy and positive attitude toward all faculty members. He assumed that every faculty member was professionally competent, displayed enthusiasm for the job and concern for student growth."

Communications

Another strong administrative characteristic distinguishing schools with good morale from those with poor morale was the form and style of communication networks used. In a suburban system with good morale, the superintendent established both formal and informal networks among various groups both within and without the schools. In a school with poor morale, the major communication system appeared to be meetings that focused primarily on academic and disciplinary problems. In a rural school with good morale, there were formal policies for ensuring good communications at all levels, within and without the school. Faculty meetings were scheduled regularly so that administrators and teachers were tuned in to what was going on.

In a comparable system with poor morale, communication from the principal was perceived as being inconsistent. In the schools with poorer morale, there seemed to be almost total reliance on formal systems of communication, for example, faculty meetings and memoranda setting forth rules. In the schools with better morale, administrators visited classrooms and talked to teachers in hallways and lounges as well as in their offices. These interchanges, as well as the generally more open nature of faculty meetings, provided administrators and teachers with more opportunities for feedback and for clearing up misperceptions.

Cliques

One of the characteristics of school systems or school buildings with relatively poor morale was the presence of cliques. These groups seemed to create a defensiveness on the part of administrators and a resulting tendency to communicate with certain groups rather than with the staff as a whole.

Sense of Mission

Extremely important to the morale of a school, according to findings from the case studies, was the articulation of a sense of mission about curriculum and the involvement of teachers and others in developing curriculum. For example, in a poor morale school the field investigators found that the district had neither a formal set of curriculum goals nor a formal philosophy of instruction. "The philosophy seemed to be: whatever works best for a given teacher is all right." In contrast, at the good morale schools, principals as instructional leaders worked closely with teachers, and their schools had a well-articulated curriculum. At one school, located in a rural environment, the superintendent was planning to introduce sex education into the curriculum for the first time. He explained to the investigator his concern about choice of words when dealing with this sensitive topic: "Words are important. We are not calling it 'sex education'." He was introducing the curriculum gradually and had arranged for the first course to be taught by one of the more respected physicians in the community.

Participation in Decision Making

None of the schools visited exhibited the participatory management style of Likert's System Four management. However, in the better morale schools, there was greater involvement of teachers in decision making, particularly in those matters that affected them professionally: curriculum development, preparing policy and student handbooks, and planning staff development programs. One teacher said that one of the more exciting activities in her teaching career was working on a self-study project.

Other teachers emphasized the need to have access to the decision-making process, whether or not they were involved in all decisions. One investigator reported that strong communication networks and the perception by teachers that they had a role in decision making, both in staff development and other areas of the school program, were extremely important for good morale. He noted that the "classroom teacher is, in many cases, an island surrounded by other islands receiving bits of data with the change of daily tides. In these days of mass communication systems, one might get the feeling that we are viewing an information overkill. Yet the fact remains it is not so much the message received that's important, but rather the individual's perception of the message that is the critical factor; and this single critical factor — the teacher's perception — most greatly affects morale."

Recognition of Teachers' Contributions

The schools with better morale generally had better systems, both formal and informal, for recognizing teachers' contributions. In the better morale schools, principals visited with teachers in hallways and lounges. They found occasions to praise individual teachers. The schools with good morale also had formal systems for recognizing teachers at PTA and faculty meetings and at graduation exercises. In schools with poor morale, such systems either did not exist or were used much less than in the better morale schools.

Discipline

In interviews in schools with poor morale, administrators and teachers often raised the issue of discipline, in contrast with those schools with good morale, where interviewers, more often than not, had to bring up the question. In the schools with better morale, there was generally a clearly written policy for students and teachers on such matters as discipline, absenteeism, tardiness, dress codes, and conduct. More often than not, in the schools with good morale, discipline codes had been developed by teams of teachers and students with considerable input from the administration.

In all of the schools, administrators agreed that they were responsible for supporting their teachers in matters of discipline and when conflicts arose with parents — a finding that contradicts reports in the media about administrative failures to enforce discipline and to support teachers. One superintendent, in discussing how he dealt with conflict between teachers and parents, stated that he was careful to get all sides of the problem — from parents, students, and teachers, separately and together. He emphasized the importance of listening to irate parents, letting them blow off steam. At the same time, he had firm guidelines about not allowing parties in the conflict to threaten or bully either himself or others involved in the conflict. He emphasized his role as listener, fact finder, and mediator. He supported teachers and other members of the staff when they were right and provided corrective direction when they were wrong, but in private without students or parents present.

Instructional and Other Support

In the schools with better morale, administrators supported teachers with instructional material, clerical help, and enforcement of discipline. In at least one system, the problem of teacher burnout was recognized and action had been taken to help teachers cope with it. This system provided teachers with counseling services designed to help them cope with burnout, financial problems, and drug and alcohol abuse.

Staff Development and Recruitment

All of the schools in the case studies had some form of staff development. However, there was considerable difference between schools with good morale and those with poor morale in the way staff development programs were conducted and planned. In the schools with better morale, teachers were very much involved in planning staff development programs. In these schools, administrators actively encouraged teachers to further their training; and as a result these schools generally have more teachers with graduate training than in the schools with poorer morale.

In those schools with good morale, principals generally played a more active part in the recruitment and selection of teachers than in schools with poorer morale. In a good morale school, the principal said, "I hand-pick my teachers and make recommendations to the central office, who make the formal offer." In a school with poorer morale, the principal reported that the personnel office recruited and selected the teachers assigned to his school.

Relationships with Board and Staff

In the schools with poor morale the school boards seemed to be more active in administrative decision making than in those schools with good morale. In those systems with good morale, superintendents seem to visit schools and to communicate more directly and openly with all personnel than they do in schools with poor morale. At the same time, they also appear to delegate more decision making to the principals, for example, on selection of teachers, staff development, and curriculum. They also seem to use formal means, such as advisory panels of administrators and teachers, to ensure building-level input into central office policy setting.

4

Improving Staff Morale:
Suggestions for Action

The numerous assumptions and research findings about morale from the literature and from our survey and case studies have been sifted and resifted to identify those variables associated with teacher morale. In this chapter these variables are translated into suggestions for action by educational leaders.

The literature on morale is massive and exceedingly murky; clear-cut conclusions are rare. Therefore, our approach to the use of research findings is a conservative one. Although we have tried to sort through this tangle of material in order to present only those suggestions in which we have faith, there is still some concern that we may not have captured the essence of the concept of morale and the conditions that affect it. For these reasons, we recommend that users of this handbook carefully assess the conditions in their school or district to determine whether the suggested practices are appropriate. Indiscriminate implementation of these suggestions is not recommended.

With these caveats in mind, we now proceed with the suggestions for educational leaders that emerged from our work. The suggestions fall into the categories in the following outline.

Outline of Suggestions for Action

1.0 Leadership and Morale
  1.1 Develop a clear concept of morale.
  1.2 Assume responsibility for establishing challenging goals.
  1.3 Involve staff in creating a vision for the unit.
  1.4 Provide material and nonmaterial support for staff.
  1.5 Provide feedback on progress toward goals.

2.0 Interpersonal Relationships and Morale

2.1 Take steps to increase job security.

2.2 Work toward establishing mutual confidence and trust.

2.3 Reduce threat and defensiveness.

2.4 Establish open channels for communication.

2.5 Reduce visible status differentials.

2.6 Exhibit behavior congruent with democratic values.

3.0 Rewards and Morale

3.1 Increase teacher responsibility.

3.2 Stress positive interactions with students as the most effective way to handle disciplinary problems.

3.3 Provide recognition for teachers' work.

3.4 Distribute rewards equitably.

3.5 Use group recognition.

3.6 Provide competitive compensatory programs but move into merit systems with caution.

4.0 Student Achievement and Morale

5.0 Workload and Morale

5.1 Establish equity in assignments.

5.2 Provide breaks for teacher rest and relaxation.

5.3 Assign teachers to their specialties and provide those teaching outside their specialties with assistance.

6.0 Facilities, Equipment, Supplies and Morale

7.0 Control Mechanisms and Morale

8.0 Professional Development and Morale

8.1 Provide opportunities for growth and development.

8.2 Base staff development programs on research findings.

8.3 Cooperatively plan faculty meetings with staff.

9.0 Extra-School Factors and Morale

9.1 Help teachers resolve personal problems.

10.0 Conflict Management and Morale

10.1 Manage conflict; don't suppress it.

1.0 Leadership and Morale

The literature clearly indicates that the leader is a key factor in determining the morale of an organization. The leader generally has the authority to arrange conditions in the environment that either foster or inhibit morale. Even though this authority is not absolute, the leader is in the best position to bring about change in the conditions affecting morale.

Leaders in school organizations with good morale have a good sense of what morale is and what seems to affect it. They have a clear vision of what they want their organizations to become and share that vision with their staff. They are ever-conscious of the staff's role in achieving the vision, and they have the motivational skills to move their staff toward the desired ends. They have and use both their positional and personal authority in positive ways to get members of the system involved in goal setting.

1.1 Develop a clear concept of morale.

The leader must develop a clear concept of morale. Although the literature is ambiguous when it comes to defining what morale is, we believe the concept encompasses the following ideas:

a. Morale is a subjective phenomenon, experienced by each member of a group in an individual way. It is something that happens in the heads of people. Each person feels the depression or euphoria brought on by external conditions, but the intensity of feeling is influenced by the personality of the individual. Although morale cannot be observed directly, the effects of good morale can be observed. Common manifestations are an eagerness to pursue the goals of a group and a willingness to withstand adversity while maintaining a "stiff upper lip."

b. Morale is a feeling that pervades the spirit of a group, much as the fragrance of flowers diffuses throughout a room. It is this feeling that causes members to defer personal satisfaction for the accomplishment of the goals of the group. It is the feeling that held the British together during the German "blitz" of London in World War II. It is the feeling that prompts people to utter, "Damn the torpedoes, full speed ahead." Manifestations of morale are most observable during times of crisis, but it is during times of calm that the foundation is laid.

c. Morale is associated with working toward worthy goals. Few of us get excited about education as a childcare function, but it is easy to get excited about eradicating illiteracy or preparing future scientists and technicians. Teachers may show little enthusiasm for their union's routine legislative lobbying efforts, but most become interested when their union defends against a cut in pay. Goals of substance stimulate members to action. According to Watson (1942), "Morale, first of all, demands a magnetic pole toward which the aspirations of men are drawn" (p. 33).

d. Morale is dynamic; it is not a permanent condition. Like a roller coaster, morale has peaks and valleys. At the present time in education, morale is at a very low point because of the unrelenting criticisms of our schools and teachers. Many teachers are alienated from their work and would leave the profession if they had the opportunity. In 1981, only 46% of the teachers in a National Education Association (1982) survey said that they would "certainly" or "probably" enter teaching again. But a decade earlier in 1971, 74% of the teachers in a similar survey indicated that they "certainly" or "probably" would enter teaching again. As conditions become more favorable to education, as criticism declines, and if financing improves, morale can be expected to climb. The hope of most leaders is to keep morale from dropping so low that it becomes detrimental to accomplishing the school's goals.

e. Morale must be considered in relation to specific groups and their goals. Morale with respect to union goals may be very high during a labor-management conflict. A union member's morale may be heightened by alleged unfair labor practices or by fear that jobs may be in jeopardy. During such a conflict, morale with respect to the organization's goals may be very low. Once the crisis is over, if the parties have negotiated fairly, the old enthusiasm for working together returns. Time, of course, may be required to heal the wounds inflicted during the confrontation.

f. Morale is the result of a complex set of environmental conditions mediated by the personal qualities of group members. Administrators should not manipulate a single variable, such as salary, and expect an automatic rise in morale. Numerous environmental and personal variables interact to affect how individuals and groups feel about exerting themselves to accomplish goals. The goals themselves, the means to the goals, the probability of achieving the goals, ownership of the goals, the nature of the leadership, and the prospect of personal reward all affect the enthusiasm with which the goals will be pursued.

The foregoing discussion of a conception of morale yields several ideas of significance to leaders. First, the leader should know that morale is a multi-dimensional concept. Leaders must take care to analyze the complementary conditions of morale. Second, the leader should know that simple one-variable manipulations are not likely to produce much of an impact on morale. Third, the leader should not be surprised if morale fluctuates widely over short periods of time because of different goals of different groups. The inconsistencies and fluctuations in morale may be baffling but no more so than the inconsistencies and fluctuations in human behavior. Fourth, the stress and guilt that leaders feel when morale plummets can be relieved by realizing that they may not have had anything at all to do with the decline. Avoidance of self-blame in such unpredictable settings is a justifiable position. And fifth, armed with this broad conception of morale, the leader can begin to work with subordinates to develop the environmental conditions that build the group's enthusiasm for achieving mutual goals.

1.2 Assume responsibility for establishing challenging goals.

Planning is essential to good morale. Staff must know where the organizational unit is going and how it will get there. Every organization must decide on the goals to be pursued, the resources required, the methods to be applied, and the procedures to be used in evaluating whether the goals are achieved. The leader is responsible for creating the process to ensure that this occurs. This does not mean that the leader does all the planning and sets all the goals. This is a sharing process involving teachers, students, parents, and other community members.

Goals are essential in educational planning. Schools without goals are schools without direction. They are adrift in a sea of conflicting demands, pushed and pulled by parents, politicians, religious zealots, and special interest groups of all persuasions. Administrative and teaching staff with well-articulated goals are capable of evaluating demands, accepting those that fit the goals and rejecting those that fall outside their mission. Goals reduce ambiguity and focus attention on what is important.

The leader's responsibility for planning involves overseeing the process by which the goals are developed, *not* doing the planning. Overseeing includes gathering data, recording minutes, and publishing and disseminating plans when they are completed. Planning must involve broad staff participation. Through such participation staff come to identify with the goals, acquire ownership in the goals, and become willing to commit energy to accomplishing the goals. Such involvement challenges the participants to stretch their capabilities and skills. When this happens, the leader may then claim success in planning.

1.3 Involve staff in creating a vision for the unit.

The leader must involve staff in creating a vision — a mission — for the unit. Involvement is a source of motivation. Staff with a voice in deciding where an organization is going and how it will get there are more committed to their work. However, motivation requires more than involvement. It is not enough for workers to be involved in setting goals. If they do not *accept* those goals, their motivation will be low. The failure to recognize this distinction causes many leaders difficulty. They go through the motions of involving staff in planning but neither listen to nor accept the input of staff. In the end it is their own goals that are pursued. When this facade of involvement is uncovered, the initial loyalty and good will generated by the involvement are eroded, and the result may be rejection of the goals.

In participative goal setting, leaders must not deny their own vision and how to realize that vision. They must be willing to advance their ideas and to argue for their acceptance. However, they must take care not to use their position of power to acquire acceptance or to cow others into accepting the leader's position. The leader's ideas must be accepted on their merit, not from a position of power.

When one involves staff in planning and goal-setting programs, one must be prepared to accept a shift in the legitimation of power. The shift is from top down to bottom up; more authority comes from the participants, less from the top administration and governing boards. While ultimate power rests with top administrators and governing boards, staff involvement, once started, cannot be arbitrarily discontinued without losses in loyalty, motivation, and morale. The authority shift must be carefully considered prior to embarking on a staff involvement program.

One way to approach involvement in planning is to set forth ground rules in

34

advance. These rules should address who will be involved, on what issues, and under what conditions; how conflicts will be resolved; and what will happen to adopted plans. Everyone should know in advance what to expect.

1.4 Provide material and nonmaterial support for staff.

The leader must provide support for the staff in accomplishing goals. Leader support may be material or nonmaterial. Material support includes the provision of space, equipment, technical and clerical assistance, supplies, books, and instructional materials. Nonmaterial support is all of those things a leader does to ease the work of staff and make the job and the workplace more pleasant. It often comes in the form of consideration for the difficulties of the job, clarifying ends and means, praising commendable performance, removing roadblocks to performance, and generally doing all of those things that help to relieve the burden as much as possible.

Material and nonmaterial support are essential for high morale. Without such support, staff feel that responsibility for goal achievement rests on their shoulders and that leaders are not carrying their fair share of the burden. Leaders must be visible and shoulder their share of the burden and help others to shoulder theirs.

1.5 Provide feedback on progress toward goals.

"How well are we doing?" is a question often asked by group members, reflecting their need to know whether the expectations for the group are being met. Without some indication of progress, there is no reason to continue striving toward a goal. When hope is gone, the leader can expect desertions from the ranks, trivial grievances, and other forms of nonproductive behavior. It is the leader's job to provide information on progress toward goals, both negative and positive. Negative feedback can boost morale when it is offered with suggestions for improvement. Positive feedback gives group members a feeling that they are on target and that success is near. Above all, feedback must be accurate. Inaccurate feedback brings disappointment and a loss in confidence and trust in the leader.

2.0 Interpersonal Relationships and Morale

The leader must have good interpersonal relationships with subordinates, patrons, and clients. Friendly relationships characterized by mutual confidence and trust are essential to high morale. Responsibility for developing these relationships rests with the leader. The leader must take the initiative; expecting others to take the first step is nonproductive. The following actions are recommended.

2.1 Take steps to increase job security.

Declining enrollment, resulting in reductions in staff, is threatening to teacher job security. This insecurity contributes to decline in morale. Teachers are understandably upset by not knowing when or if their positions will be abolished. Leaders must take steps to reduce the anxiety of reduction-in-force actions. Even with tenure, positions may be abolished in times of retrenchment. Such steps should include a clear and equitable reduction-in-force policy, an income and health insurance maintenance program, and a fair layoff-recall system. These security provisions will clearly communicate that leaders are concerned about the welfare of followers.

2.2 Work toward establishing mutual confidence and trust.

Maintaining effective interpersonal relations requires mutual confidence and trust. Where these exist, the parties to a relationship all feel that each is contributing to the achievement of the unit's goals. When hard times come, all perceive that each is suffering equally. When good times prevail, all perceive that each shares equally in the abundance.

A number of American industries experienced a loss in mutual confidence and trust during the recent recession. While workers were asked to sacrifice wages and benefits to keep their organizations afloat, the managers were being given raises or bonuses. Sacrifice was unequal; confidence and trust were severely strained; morale plummeted. To overcome these problems, some of these industries cut managerial salaries, withheld bonuses, and reduced perks to demonstrate that all employees were sacrificing equally. In these cases, the results were smoother union-management relationships, more reasonable employee demands during subsequent negotiations, and improved morale overall.

Leaders must be willing to sacrifice right along with teachers during times of financial crises. If teachers must go without supplies and materials, so must their leaders. The cars provided to leaders can be compacts rather than gas guzzlers. The administrative office staff can be trimmed and trips to conferences and conventions reduced. Such sacrifices demonstrate the willingness of leaders to share in the hardships being experienced by the school system. Confidence and trust are built by such actions. When leaders and staff feel that they are operating under the same conditions, they develop a sense of partnership in the organization and become psychologically close to each other.

2.3 Reduce threat and defensiveness.

Leaders must realize that damage to interpersonal relationships occurs whenever individuals experience threats to their self-concepts, their positions, their beliefs, or their possessions. Defensiveness is a natural response to threat. It is manifested in fight or flight behavior, both of which contribute to loss of morale.

Fight behavior may be physical, but in our society it usually takes the form of political infighting or various forms of getting even. Courts are full of litigants, political action committees are formed to fight for a cause, petitions circulate freely, and school board meetings are preoccupied with handling complaints. Collective action is a favored means of protest. "Throw the bums out of office" is an American tradition.

Flight behavior is manifested by leaving the "field of battle," giving in to the demands of others, forfeiting one's position, or giving up one's property. Flight behavior is manifested when school leaders try to pacify critics by accepting their criticisms without adequate study, dialogue, or refutation. It may seem far easier at the moment of the threat to give in, to give up, or to forfeit something than it is to take a stand and fight it out. However, it may be extremely costly in the long run.

Threats to cherished values, such as equality, fairness, honesty, justice, and freedom, will likely lead to defensive reactions. Teachers and administrators are expected to display these values, for the school is perceived as a microcosm of the ideal democratic society. Their behavior is more closely scrutinized by the public, and they must hold themselves to a higher standard of conduct with respect to these values than other citizens. When they fail, patrons believe that educators have let society down, and the fight or flight reactions set in. Such reactions are manifested in the increase in public criticism, the issuance of national reports by various commissions, talk of tax credits and vouchers, and the flight to private schools.

2.4 Establish open channels for communication.

School leaders must communicate openly and regularly in a form that is appropriate to patrons, clients, peers, and superiors. Content must be understandable and in a form that attracts the attention of the receiver. It must not be propaganda; it must treat real issues and present them fairly.

2.5 Reduce visible status differentials.

Although differential status items are the rewards of office, leaders must take care not to flaunt these rewards. It is best to keep status differentials as invisible as possible. Special parking spaces, expensive office furnishings, a number of assistants, a large expense account, a furnished automobile, and an air-conditioned office others do not have create a psychological gap between leaders and staff. Keeping status differentials to a minimum helps to improve interpersonal relationships.

2.6 Exhibit behavior congruent with democratic values.

School leaders must exemplify the ideals of a democratic society. They must treat all people as equals regardless of race, sex, age, or national origin. They must avoid racial, ethnic, and sexist jokes and allusions. They must exemplify fairness in their judgments, never allowing personal friendship to intrude on their decisions. They must be above petty thievery and misuse of school funds, property, and personnel. Stationery, phones, stamps, secretarial time, vehicles, and equipment must never be used for personal purposes. Justice must prevail in solving conflicts. Punishment must serve a legitimate purpose and must be commensurate with the infraction. In daily interactions with staff, students, and community members, the leader must demonstrate sensitivity to their feelings and conditions of life. These values are basic and as such must be practiced by the leaders of educational institutions. Failure to uphold these values is viewed as a failure of the institution and results in loss of support and confidence in that institution.

Leaders must be ever aware of interpersonal relationships and the subtle factors that affect them. When conflict, mistrust, lack of confidence, and miscommunication exist, morale is affected negatively. Leaders must take responsibility for developing human relationships that enhance the good feelings that people have for accomplishing the unit's goals.

3.0 Rewards and Morale

The primary rewards of teaching are more psychic than material. This does not mean that teachers are not interested in material rewards; it is simply stating a fact of life in the teaching profession. Psychic rewards result from being appreciated for doing one's work well, from developing programs for students, and from observing student learning and knowing that one has had a hand in it. These rewards also come from knowing that one is an important and worthwhile person in the minds of friends and fellow associates.

Material rewards are concerned with the security of one's person and family, both now and in the future. Dollars earned and benefits secured are important material rewards. Such material rewards have always been scarce in the field of education. Therefore, psychic rewards become all the more important. Following are some actions leaders may take to enhance teachers' psychic rewards.

3.1 Increase teacher responsibility.

Leaders must prevent bureaucratic centralization that removes autonomy for instruction from classroom teachers. Imposing lockstep procedures for teaching any subject must be avoided. Respecting the teacher's competence may be enhanced by 1) reducing inspection-type supervision; 2) providing a variety of curricular resources so teachers can select those appropriate to the needs of students; 3) not letting textbook and test companies govern what is taught in classrooms; 4) not requiring teachers to cover a certain number of pages, skills, or concepts by a given time of the year; and 5) not comparing the quantity of work completed by teacher A with that of teacher B. If the school is viewed as a professional institution and not a bureaucracy, teachers should have the autonomy to make instructional decisions necessary to perform their work in a competent and rewarding way.

3.2 Stress positive interactions with students as the most effective way to handle disciplinary problems.

Teaching has both its satisfactions and dissatisfactions. Satisfaction comes from helping students learn. It comes from the student who returns to express appreciation for something the teacher said or did that had an impact on the student's life. It comes from observing the successes of former students in business, the professions, athletics, or the arts. It comes from knowing that what the teacher did touched someone's life in a meaningful and important way. Dissatisfaction in teaching comes when there are too many disciplinary problems both inside and outside the classroom. The constant press of these problems leads to burnout, and the result is lowered morale.

Student discipline is a long-standing problem in our schools. Many effective approaches to discipline stressing positive interactions with students are found in *Handbook for Developing Schools with Good Discipline* by the Phi Delta Kappa Commission on Discipline (1982). All school systems need to develop and implement a firm and fair disciplinary plan. Administrators must share this responsibility with teachers. Teachers must be assured that administrators will support them when dealing with habitual offenders and dangerous or emotionally disturbed students, removing them from classrooms when necessary. Such support communicates to teachers that their professional judgment is accepted and acted upon.

3.3 Provide recognition for teachers' work.

School leaders must serve as models to students, parents, and peers in providing recognition of teachers' work. All should be encouraged to write, telephone, or directly convey their personal feelings about worthy contributions of teachers. Such private means of communication bolster teachers' feelings of self-worth. Such communications do not have to be shared; their value comes from the personal recognition of a job well done. Recognition, both personal and public, is a powerful morale builder. When teachers are valued, they feel good about themselves, about their work, and about others.

3.4 Distribute rewards equitably.

Rewards can contribute to morale when those receiving them believe that they are distributed equitably. However, equity does not mean equality. If rewards are distributed indiscriminately, there is no equity. If those deserving them and those not deserving them are treated equally, rewards are meaningless and their morale value is lost.

3.5 Use group recognition.

Administrators should encourage PTAs, teacher associations, administrator organizations, the school board, and civic groups, among others, to recognize teachers as a group. These efforts let teachers know that their work is not going unnoticed, that they are important people in the lives of the emerging generation, and that their work is an essential part of American economic and social life. No teacher needs to be singled out on such occasions. All can bask in the warmth of the recognition.

3.6 Provide competitive compensatory programs but move into merit systems with caution.

Although much has been written on the relationship between compensation and morale, it is not possible to state definitive conclusions at this time. However, a few tentative generalizations may be stated.

Workers seem to be sensitive to their financial position relative to others. Hoppock (1977) cited the case of one worker who had a low income compared to national averages, but his income was relatively high compared to that of his friends and neighbors. The worker was satisfied with his income. His relatively high income gave him status in the eyes of those who were important to him. The national averages did not seem to matter. This example has some parallels in education. Teachers who are relatively well paid in their community probably feel good about themselves, their jobs, and their community. If they are poorly paid relative to others in their community, morale is likely to be low.

Teacher associations and government agencies publicize average salaries and salary schedules for individual states and for the nation. Most teachers know where they rank relative to teachers in other districts. They also know that the cost of living differs from community to community and from state to state. Morale becomes an issue when teachers realize that their total compensatory package is considerably lower than that of nearby school systems similar in size, wealth, and other qualities.

Workers also are concerned about potential future earnings relative to present compensation. One is often willing to accept a low-paying position if the potential for future earnings is good. Most teacher salary schedules do not provide this potential. In teaching, compensation is front-loaded, yearly increments are small, and salary at retirement may be only twice that of entering teachers (Lortie 1975). Because of these conditions, compensation frequently becomes a negative morale factor.

Merit pay and other differential reward programs have come out of the closet once again. Although teachers believe that those who are more effective in the classroom should receive larger salary increases than those who are less effective (Rist 1983), teacher organizations oppose such programs on the ground that their negative effects outweigh their positive returns. Such plans cannot be fairly administered, they say. Teacher evaluation systems lack objectivity, thus permitting gross errors in judgment of quality, they claim. Further, they say that the evaluators are not competent to judge teaching. Many have been away from the classroom too long to know what teaching is like these days, and content has changed so rapidly in some fields that the administrator can not judge whether the teacher is up-to-date. These limitations of merit systems are said to contribute to dissension, jealousies, and a general decline in morale.

Proponents argue that merit systems permit equity in compensation and enhance the quality of education by rewarding excellence in teaching. They claim administrators are competent to judge the educational process; they know how learning is facilitated, and they can determine when a teacher is doing a good job. Proponents claim that knowledge of content is not necessary to the evaluation of the teaching process.

Researchers of merit pay systems during the late 1950s (Mathis 1959; Chandler 1959; Carpenter 1959) found that teacher morale did not differ in merit and nonmerit school systems. However, care must be exercised in interpreting Mathis' results, because both groups of schools had salary schedules well above the national average and both schedules were quite similar throughout the range of salaries. Carpenter did find that those school systems in which teachers had cooperatively developed the merit plan had higher morale than those systems that did not involve teachers.

Merit systems must be approached with caution. There have been numerous failures. David Lipsky (quoted by McCurdy 1984) found that merit pay systems tend to have a common history: "In the first couple of years it's greeted with enthusiasm from everybody. . . . Then the problems start. . . . Jealousies develop; morale declines. Administrators [are] put in the hot seat. . . . It's usually dropped after five or six years" (p. 146). Robinson's (1984) review of 239 merit system failures revealed the following reasons for their demise: unsatisfactory evaluative criteria and procedures, administrative problems, staff dissension, restrictive cutoffs, inadequate financial backing, failure to gain the consent of teachers, lack of definition of superior results, and inability to measure results (pp. 4-5). The first three above were also noted by Calhoun and Protheroe (1983) as the chief reasons for dropping merit systems.

Despite the literature on merit system failures, there are some success stories as well (McCurdy 1984). Successful systems, according to Robinson (1984), tend to have several common characteristics: adequate base salaries, objective and consistently applied assessment measures, effective evaluation procedures, well-defined educational objectives, effective student assessment measures, board and management commitment, staff involvement in program development, a plausible definition of superior performance, valid measures of results, workable administrative procedures, the promotion of teacher satisfaction and cooperation, adequate funding to cover all who qualify, the promotion of student learning, and a plan for continuous evaluation of the merit system itself (pp. 19-22).

The effectiveness of evaluators in carrying out their responsibilities seems to be a crucial element in the success of merit plans. Evaluators are provided careful training and given sufficient assistance to enable them to spend the required time in collecting the data needed to make well-documented evaluations. In Ladue, Missouri, evaluators spend 15 to 20 hours per teacher each year in evaluating performance (McCurdy 1984). School districts that plan to move into merit systems must be willing to spend the resources necessary to permit this intensive involvement in teacher evaluation by administrators.

When considering merit systems, administrators should be aware of the variety of plans that have been tried. Some are based on student achievement gains, others on teacher performance. In the former, when student gains by class or building are assessed, teachers, individually or as a group, are given merit increases. In the latter, expectations for individual teacher performance are established and rated. Merit is based on the ratings. Controversy surrounds both approaches and, at present, which one is used appears to be based on the personal preferences of those developing the system.

The current interest in merit systems has resulted in new concepts and new terms. Houston has its Second-Mile Plan; Midland, Tex., and Charlotte, N.C., have a career ladder, and one is being implemented statewide in Tennessee; California has a teacher-mentor plan; and there are a variety of other merit pay systems. McCurdy (1984) has classified the approaches to merit into three groups: performance-based merit pay systems, master teacher plans, and career-ladder plans. In master teacher plans additional pay is based on demonstrated competence, while in career-ladder plans additional pay is based on extra duties, additional responsibilities, professional growth, teaching in shortage areas, and the like.

The best advice we can offer at the present time is for administrators to move into merit systems mindful of the failures and the successes. They must negotiate the pitfalls with due care because the odds against success are great. They must take each step with caution, bringing teachers, parents, administrators, and the board of education with them. The process must be open to inspection and to broad participation. Commitment of funds, time, and energy is essential. Believing that a workable merit system can be developed and implemented is crucial. This is not a project for the faint of heart.

4.0 Student Achievement and Morale

There is a positive correlation between high student achievement and high teacher morale. However, one cannot assume direct cause-and-effect relationship from a positive correlation. Good morale may cause teachers to put more effort into their work, thereby producing high student achievement; or the high student achievement may cause teachers to feel good about themselves and their work, thereby producing high morale. Regardless of the direction of causality, administrators and teachers should strive to increase both student achievement and morale since both are highly desirable qualities in any school system.

One recent piece of evidence supporting the relationship between morale and student achievement is provided by Hopkins-Layton (1981). She found a positive relationship between student achievement gains in the previous year and teacher attendance. Although this was correlational evidence, it has a very practical implication. For purely economic reasons, administrators should develop incentives for teachers to avoid taking days off. Some districts are paying for unused sick leave when teachers leave or retire. Others are providing special recognition for teachers who miss only a few days. Houston has set a maximum number of days that can be missed for those who wish to participate in its Second-Mile Plan. Besides being financially sound, such plans are also sound educationally. The experience of many substitutes is that they spend so much time on discipline that there is not much left to proceed with the regular program of instruction. The substitute's presence is often little more than babysitting.

5.0 Workload and Morale

Inequity in assignments can contribute to a decline in teacher morale. Teachers who do things well tend to be called on more frequently to perform extra duties. Often, their only reward is a "thank you" from the administrator. There are other teachers who grumble about any extra or special assignments and do the minimum they can to get by. As a result, the administrator tends to avoid asking these teachers to take on extra assignments. The inequity of such circumstances does not escape the attention of the willing workers. If the inequity persists, a morale problem is likely to surface.

5.1 Establish equity in assignments.

Assignment inequities can occur in a number of areas within a school or in a district. They include the number of students in a class; the types of students, particularly those with exceptionalities requiring inordinate amounts of time and emotional energy; monitoring corridors, lunch rooms, lavatories, parking lots, bus loading areas, and study halls; working on committees requiring extensive after-hours preparation; supervising unpaid extracurricular activities; advisement responsibilities; and the number of separate lesson preparations. The administrator should periodically review each teacher's workload; where inequities are noted, they must be corrected.

However, correcting inequities must be done with due care. Many teachers have made a considerable investment in the special projects they have been assigned. They have acquired materials, contacts, skills, and knowledge that allow them to carry out the project effectively. Removing the project from the teacher's responsibility means a loss of this investment. Whenever changes are being considered for these special assignments, the administrator should discuss the change with the teacher and assess the loss to the teacher before the change is consummated. This is less important, of course, when trivial duties are involved.

5.2 Provide breaks for teacher rest and relaxation.

Maslach and Pines (1977) have pointed out the impact that intense interaction with children in a child-care center has on the staff's feelings about their jobs. In centers with high child/staff ratios, the staff spent more hours in direct contact with children, fewer hours in staff meetings, and took fewer vacations. They felt less free to take a break when they felt they needed one. Unable to express themselves freely on the job and without any input into the center's policies, they felt alienated from their work and without control over their jobs. They were more likely to sanction compulsory naps and sedatives for hyperactive children. As they came to like their jobs less, they became more critical in their evaluations of the center.

Maslach and Pines also found that the number of hours at work is not in itself a good predictor of staff feelings about their work and about children. It is the number of hours in direct contact with children that is the potent indicator. Those staff members who did administrative work worked longer hours than those who worked with children, but they did not have the same negative feelings as those who spent the full day with young children. They had more positive feelings about children, the center, and the relationships between staff and parents. These feelings seem to be associated with the freedom, flexibility, and control over their time. However, some deterioration in patience, cheerfulness, and fairness was noted in the behavior of these administrators toward the end of the day.

A variable that appears to be associated with intense child contact is the structure of the program in which one is involved. Again, Maslach and Pines found that workers in relatively unstructured programs felt better about their work than those in structured programs. However, even these workers "reported a greater change in emotional feelings (from high to low) and said they were much less cheerful, less tolerant, less intimate, less idealistic, less alert, less playful, and more moody and irritable than they had been at the beginning of the day" (p. 109).

An open or unstructured program requires workers to live in an environment that bombards them with multiple stimuli at any one time, each requiring a different response from the worker. An analogy may be the air traffic controller who must be aware of levels, distances, numbers and types of aircraft, destinations, and directions. At any moment other aircraft may be added and some may leave or land. Emergencies may arise at any time; and requests to change speed, direction, altitude, and destination demand quick responses. Such an environment requires intense concentration and constant mental activity. Whether an air traffic controller or a child-care worker, one can understand the "let down" at the day's end resulting from emotional and physical exhaustion.

Administrators must be aware of and sensitive to the physical and emotional exhaustion experienced by teachers. Teachers need breaks every day. These may be provided during recess supervised by aides, through creative scheduling of special teachers (art, music, physical education), use of volunteers or aides in the classroom, or through other scheduling innovations. In addition, arrangements should be made for teacher "time-out." Administrators will need to do some creative scheduling or occasionally provide class coverage personally when a teacher feels a need for a break from the classroom. The more open the program, the more important it is to provide time-out for teachers.

Breaks, time-out, and free periods must not be given grudgingly as if they were wasted on idle chatter in the teachers' lounge. They must be considered a source of renewal for the teacher — a time to relax, to be away from students, to be with other adults, or to be alone. Teachers should be free to do whatever they wish during this time — it is their professional free time. Administrators must protect this time from criticism by external sources and educate these critics as to why it is important for the mental health of teachers.

5.3 Assign teachers to their specialties and provide those teaching outside their specialties with assistance.

In areas of teacher shortages, and especially in small school districts, teachers often are asked to take assignments that are outside their fields of certification. Such assignments can be a source of considerable stress and frustration. Much additional time is required for lesson preparations; evaluations of performance may be lower; and one's sense of competence may be undermined. If conditions require such assignments, administrators must be prepared to provide the additional support these teachers require. These teachers should be encouraged to become certified as rapidly as possible through such incentives as tuition stipends, inservice grants, or arranging for needed courses to be taught within the district or within a reasonable commuting distance. Evaluations of performance must be honest but must take into consideration the fact that the teacher is not working in his area of specialization. Extra duties should be kept to a minimum during the early days of the assignment. These may be added as the teacher increases in competence and confidence.

Some evidence is available to indicate a positive association between being assigned to teach in one's college major and morale (Nimmer 1979). It seems reasonable that if teachers have spent four or more years studying a field, they will approach the field with confidence and enthusiasm. In addition, preparation time is reduced, feelings of effectiveness are higher, and the likelihood of favorable evaluations is greater (Passarella 1978). Under such conditions teacher morale should be higher. Therefore, assignments should match the teacher's college major as closely as possible.

6.0 Facilities, Equipment, Supplies and Morale

One of the frustrating conditions experienced by teachers is to be asked to do their work with outdated equipment and textbooks, inadequate supplies, and poor facilities. A room, desks, textbooks, and a chalkboard are no longer adequate for an effective instructional program. In many places teachers must still scrounge for materials. They seek used paper from businesses and public agencies. They purchase their own duplicating masters. Clerical assistance is seldom available. Resourceful teachers take up the challenge and search for materials from all sources. Others, however, may become disenchanted because the district fails to provide the support required to implement an adequate program.

Leaders must be aware of teacher needs for facilities, equipment, supplies, and clerical assistance, and provide for these needs, if possible, in the regular district budget. When the budget falls short, many leaders have become experts in locating new sources of money. They run sales, carnivals, and raffles; they write grant proposals; they solicit contributions of materials, equipment, and expertise from businesses.

7.0 Control Mechanisms and Morale

Control is a necessary function in any organization. One enters into both psychological and legal contracts when one becomes a member of an organization. The member agrees to pursue the organization's goals; the organization agrees to reward the member with certain desired benefits. Beyond the legal contract, both parties use various methods to control the behavior of the other. Among them are threat of severing the relationship, withholding benefits, psychological pressure, periodic evaluations, formal orientations and ceremonies, promulgation of rules and regulations, and finely tuned communication systems.

In schools all of these methods are used to control teacher behavior. Until a teacher acquires tenure, the threat of nonrenewal is ever present. Even with tenure, teachers are faced with periodic evaluations based on school district expectations. The result could be termination, probation, reprimand, reassignment, or some other administrative action. Peers also pressure colleagues into behaving in ways acceptable to them. Parents have their expectations as well, and they also bring pressure to bear on teachers. Whenever a teacher gets too far out of line, the administrator may call a conference to communicate and reinforce the expectations of the school system. Faculty meetings are used to communicate and reinforce norms of behavior for teachers as a group. All of these mold teachers' behavior into acceptable patterns. Some are subtle, others are blatant attempts to bring about conformity.

Teachers, as a professional group, have a code of conduct separate from that of the school system. It is enforced by peer pressure. Self-control and self-direction are considered professional prerogatives. Bureaucratic school systems, however, have never permitted these prerogatives to be exercised. Evaluation and control are exercised by administrators, not teachers and their organizations. The result has been a professional-bureaucratic conflict that has never been resolved, even in states where unions have increased teacher power. Control remains in the hands of administrators.

If school leaders wish to increase teacher morale, they must begin to treat teachers as professionals. Teachers should have a greater role in determining what is taught, how it is taught, and when it is taught. They should be evaluated less frequently when they are tenured. They should be helped to develop the mechanisms for purging the unfit from their ranks. They should be involved in the induction, orientation, and socialization of new professionals so they can become self-directing. As teachers assume these professional roles, the bureaucratic rules and regulations can be withdrawn or drastically reduced.

Some may think that teacher self-control is utopian nonsense. It is if teachers are not properly prepared for their professional responsibilities. The substitution of professional control for bureaucratic control in the teaching profession will take some time. And when that time comes, the profession will be more able to attract the brightest to its ranks.

8.0 Professional Development and Morale

Improving teacher effectiveness requires that staff development be provided by the school district. Through inservice programs and other staff development activities, teachers can improve their knowledge and skills, thus enhancing their feelings about themselves and their morale. Administrators also need such opportunities for professional growth. They should include time in their schedules for attending conferences, reading, and maintaining contact with the literature in their field.

8.1 Provide opportunities for growth and development.

Healthy individuals seek opportunities for growth and development. Through these opportunities, teachers develop competence, confidence, self-esteem, and the feeling that they are fulfilling their potential. The result is satisfaction with self, work, and others. Inservice education is a means to these desired ends.

Successful inservice programs have a number of characteristics. First, teachers are closely involved in planning, implementing, and evaluating the program. The more teacher involvement the more likely the inservice program will provide the kinds of experience that will enhance their personal and professional development.

Second, the inservice program is viewed as an important part of the education program in the school district. The board of education has a written policy on inservice programs; an item is included in the budget for the program; and a staff member is responsible and accountable for administering the program. Activities are held during normal working hours. When this is not possible, compensatory leave or pay is provided.

Third, the program starts with the expectation that the development of teachers' potential will result in improvement in the quality of instruction. Funds for inservice programs are treated as an investment with a high rate of return in improved student learning.

Fourth, the program provides opportunities for both group and individual growth. Teachers are able to select from a number of alternatives depending on their needs. Where feasible, paid consultants are made available for demonstrations, coaching, and private consultations on individual professional problems. Where funds are not available, central office personnel and qualified teachers in the system perform these functions. Group inservice programs are targeted on one area at a time. Participants are saturated in this one area before another target is selected.

Fifth, the inservice program is based on research. Emphasis is given to those practices that have the greatest empirical support. Only through conscious efforts to use research-based knowledge will educators improve the quality of education and the status of the profession.

8.2 Base staff development programs on research findings.

Current research about effective staff development programs (see Sparks 1983) is supportive of the above suggestions. In general the goals of staff development programs are to fine tune existing teacher skills or to introduce teachers to new skills and concepts. Sparks has identified key elements in staff development programs that are empirically related to teacher behavior change. The following activities should be considered to maximize program effectiveness.

First, the program must create an awareness level that encourages the teacher to want to change. Second, along with the informational content, effective staff development programs must provide demonstrations, including live modeling, videotaping, and detailed narrative descriptions. Allen (1984) found that demonstrations preceded by information sessions are considerably more effective in bringing about change than information sessions alone, demonstrations alone, or demonstrations followed by information sessions. Third, small discussion groups with a group leader have been identified as necessary to bring about the acceptance of change and to maintain the momentum of change. Finally, teachers must be given opportunities to practice the desired change and to receive feedback on their performance. Format of the feedback could include microteaching, role playing, and peer observation (Sparks 1983, pp. 67-70).

Teaching demands excellence if it is to be a true profession. It is unrealistic to expect that the preservice training of teachers is adequate to achieve this excellence. Providing inservice and staff development programs is one way school leaders can ensure excellence.

8.3 Cooperatively plan faculty meetings with staff.

Faculty meetings provide opportunities for staff to share many matters with their colleagues. They do not have to have a rigid agenda, nor do they always have to include all members of the staff. Grade-level meetings, team meetings, or departmental meetings often are preferable because they are more informal and permit more sharing and conferring about common problems. Such meetings offer opportunities for mutual support and remove the feeling of isolation many teachers have. Teachers learn from such meetings that they are not alone in the problems they face and that there are alternative ways of coping with their problems.

Teachers prefer meetings dealing with issues that affect their work. They want to discuss parental problems, discipline, student learning difficulties, and curriculum topics; they want to check their views with colleagues whose judgments they respect; and they want the social-emotional support of their peers. Staff meetings can provide opportunities for these kinds of participation, sharing, and social-emotional support.

Faculty meetings do not have to be dominated by the administrator. A committee of faculty and the administrator can plan meetings that meet the needs of teachers. Such involvement will remove the common gripe of teachers that faculty meetings are too long, often irrelevant, and unproductive.

9.0 Extra-School Factors and Morale

Roach (1958) has noted that employees have an overall attitude that affects all aspects of their work. If this attitude is positive, there is a tendency for the employee to like all aspects of the job; if it is negative, the employee tends to dislike all aspects of the job. If illness, marital problems, financial problems, or problems with children cause a person to become depressed, this depression carries over to the work setting. The person may be unable to concentrate on the job, productivity may decline, relationships with superiors and peers may deteriorate, and one's self-confidence and feelings of competence may wane. All are conditions that can contribute to negative feelings and poor morale. Leaders are coming to recognize that if they can help their subordinates to resolve or cope with problems, their efforts will pay large dividends. A good example of how an elementary principal worked with his teachers, students, and parents on their personal problems is described by Hirsch (1983).

9.1 Help teachers resolve personal problems.

School systems can learn from the example of business, which has many programs for helping employees with personal problems. Counseling services or referral services should be made available to people who have problems with alcohol, drugs, family relationships, and finances. Larger school districts may want to provide the services directly; smaller districts may use a referral system. In either case, the school district should be willing to pick up all or part of the cost of the program. A three-way cost split might be negotiated among the teacher, the teacher association, and the school district. Privacy rights of employees seeking treatment must be protected.

10.0 Conflict Management and Morale

Conflict is inevitable in human relationships. Traditionally, the approach of management has been to avoid conflict situations. More recently, however, conflict is being recognized and accepted as a healthy aspect of human interaction. According to Rahim (1976), conflict is essential to productivity and change. Doolittle (1976) has found conflict to be a stimulus for the examination and resolution of problems; an opportunity to teach people about their personal values, abilities, and limitations; and a source of motivation.

10.1 Manage conflict; don't suppress it.

The traditional approach to conflict in schools has been either to avoid it or to suppress it. Either strategy results in a seething undercurrent of tension between teachers and administrators that is destructive to morale.

Derr (1972) believes that conflicts stem from many sources and become pervasive throughout the organization. Because the origin of conflicts is random in complex organizations, the conflict management strategy will depend on the situation. However, there are steps that can be taken to manage conflicts arising in complex organizations: 1) provide administrators with training in resolving various types of conflicts, 2) intervene by changing the existing structures of the organization to divert the occurrence of conflict among workers, and 3) anticipate problems that breed destructive conflicts and resolve them by evaluating the organization and remediating the problems before the conflicts arise.

Managing interpersonal conflict is essentially managing individual differences among people. Interpersonal conflict typically follows four stages: 1) anticipation of an impending situation, 2) conscious but unexpressed differences among people that result in a build-up of tension and feelings of impending trouble, 3) discussion of differences of opinions, and 4) open conflict and dispute with strongly held points of view. The administrator will have greater success in managing conflict if intervention occurs at the earlier stages. Some of the approaches to managing interpersonal conflicts are third-party intervention, coaching and counseling, process training, and appeal systems.

In third-party intervention the administrator serves as a mediator to help the parties involved to resolve the immediate conflict, to gain control over the events that led to the conflict, and to develop resources to treat future conflict more effectively. Third-party mediators can isolate the adversaries' arguments, separating the real issues from the peripheral ones. They also can overcome a win-lose outcome by offering face-saving strategies.

When the use of a mediator is neither appropriate nor feasible, the administrator can effectively deal with interpersonal conflicts by using coaching and counseling. By being a good listener, the administrator gains empathy and understanding of how the individuals involved perceive the conflict. By listening, the administrator enables the participants in a conflict to talk through the dispute in a nonthreatening atmosphere. Often the administrator gains insight into ways of making changes in the organization to avoid future conflicts.

Another way for an administrator to respond to interpersonal conflicts is to help the parties involved increase their awareness of the processes that led to the conflict rather than focusing on the specific content of the conflict. Such enriched awareness by the conflicting parties provides a better base for understanding the conflict and contributes to its resolution.

In addition to the informal strategies described above, there are such formalized procedures as the appeal process to manage conflict. The formal appeal process supplements but does not supplant the informal methods. The organization's leaders set the tone of the appeal system. It can be benevolent or controlling; or it can be compromising, whereby a settlement is negotiated that is acceptable to both employer and employee. The criteria for settlement may be from legal statutes, board policies, or standards set by the adjudicator hearing the case.

Intergroup conflict situations also occur in school organizations. Like interpersonal conflict, intergroup conflict results when disagreement occurs across groups or when group interests compete. Mistrust and closed communications are common features of intergroup conflict.

Managing intergroup conflict is usually more formalized than managing interpersonal conflict. When negotiation, mediation, and arbitration result in win-lose situations, there is often an aftermath of serious problems, with the administrator left to patch up feelings after a decision has been made.

How conflict is managed can be a critical element in a staff's morale. Leaders themselves are sometimes party to a conflict, but more typically their role is to manage conflict. For leaders, managing conflict goes with the job; it takes a good amount of tolerance and patience.

Morale is a complex matter. Manipulating a single variable won't do the job. From the many action suggestions provided, school leaders can choose those that best fit the conditions of their systems. Our hope is that implementing at least some of these suggestions will have a positive impact on the morale of educators in the school systems throughout the country.

5

Assessing Your Potential
for Facilitating Staff Morale

From the action suggestions for improving morale reported in Chapter 4, we have developed a diagnostic instrument for assessing leaders' strengths and weaknesses in facilitating the morale of their staffs. We call the instrument "Inventory of Leaders' Potential for Facilitating Staff Morale." We use the phrase "potential for facilitating staff morale" because there is insufficient research to establish a direct cause-and-effect relationship between what a leader does and its effect on subordinates' morale. However, there are a large number of leader behaviors, attitudes, and skills that *appear* to have some relationship to morale on the basis of correlational research, practice, and conventional wisdom. These behaviors, attitudes, and skills are reflected in the items in the inventory. Researchers should be aware that this inventory has not been subjected to empirical tests of validity and reliability, but we do believe it has surface validity.

The 10 sections in the inventory are coordinated with the 10 sections of suggestions for action in Chapter 4. Not all points discussed in Chapter 4 are included as items in the inventory. However, a sufficient number have been included to provide a useful self-rating scale of a leader's potential for facilitating morale.

Each item requires respondents to indicate how often (never, seldom, usually, always) they exhibit the behavior, use the skill, or hold the attitude expressed in the statement. A fifth category, "not applicable," may be used when conditions do not permit one of the other responses. Items so marked are omitted in calculating a score.

A copy of the complete inventory follows; a score sheet is provided as an appendix.

Inventory of Leaders' Potential for Facilitating Staff Morale

Directions: Read each item carefully and circle the response that indicates the extent to which you exhibit the behavior, use the skill, or hold the attitude expressed in the statement. Be as honest as possible in recording your response.

Possible responses	Code
Never	N
Seldom	S
Usually	U
Always	A
Not Applicable	NA

1.0 Leadership

1. I am concerned about how my subordinates feel about their work.   N S U A NA

2. I let my superiors know how their subordinates feel about their work.   N S U A NA

3. I am sensitive to fluctuations in my subordinates' morale.   N S U A NA

4. I note things that are associated with fluctuations in my subordinates' morale.   N S U A NA

5. I set standards that challenge my subordinates.   N S U A NA

6. I involve my subordinates in setting or changing the mission, goals, and objectives of the unit.   N S U A NA

7. I work hard to provide the material resources needed by my subordinates to do their work well.   N S U A NA

8. I willingly praise subordinates for doing their work well.   N S U A NA

9. I keep my subordinates apprised of how well they are doing.   N S U A NA

2.0 Interpersonal Relationships

10. I keep my subordinates apprised of conditions that may affect the security of their jobs.   N S U A NA

11. I help subordinates who are RIFed to locate other positions.   N S U A NA

12. I believe that my subordinates do excellent work.   N S U A NA

13. I ask subordinates if I am handling my job well.   N S U A NA

14. My subordinates feel free to talk with me about professional and personal problems.   N S U A NA

15. I feel free to discuss my professional and personal problems with my subordinates.   N S U A NA

16. I seek interaction with staff members.   N S U A NA

17. I encourage teachers to seek interaction with other staff members.   N S U A NA

18. I avoid such personal privileges as a parking slot that is off-limits to my subordinates.   N S U A NA

19. I am honest in my dealings with others.   N S U A NA

3.0 Rewards

20. I give my subordinates a free hand in their work.   N S U A NA

21. When I assign tasks, I let my subordinates do the work without interference from me.   N S U A NA

22. I handle disciplinary problems promptly.   N S U A NA

23. I handle subordinates' requests with dispatch.   N S U A NA

24. I use many methods of rewarding subordinates for excellence.   N S U A NA

25. I reward those who achieve excellence and avoid rewarding those who achieve only mediocre results.   N S U A NA

26. I use group rewards from time to time.   N S U A NA

27. I support a salary system based on an equitable distribution of pay for the achievement of results.   N S U A NA

28. I encourage others to let my subordinates know when they are doing a good job.   N S U A NA

4.0 Student Achievement

29. I emphasize student achievement in my unit.   N S U A NA

30. I communicate to my subordinates that student achievement is the primary goal of the unit.   N S U A NA

5.0 Workload

31. I distribute the workload equitably among my subordinates.   N S U A NA

32. I make assignments based on the training and skills of my subordinates.   N S U A NA

33. I permit subordinates to take breaks from their work without my permission.   N S U A NA

34. I check to be sure that my subordinates are not overloaded.   N S U A NA

6.0 Facilities, Equipment, and Supplies

35. I involve my staff in selecting supplies and equipment needed to do their work.   N S U A NA

36. I make sure that the staff lounge is a pleasant place to spend breaks.   N S U A NA

37. I make sure that materials and equipment available to my subordinates are up-to-date.   N S U A NA

38. I make sure there are sufficient quantities of materials and equipment for all staff members.   N S U A NA

39. I work to make the facilities attractive and clean.   N S U A NA

40. I work hard to provide the materials, equipment, and facilities needed by my subordinates.   N S U A NA

7.0 Control Mechanisms

41. I use peer pressure to regulate subordinates' behavior.   N S U A NA

42. I appeal to subordinates' feelings of fairness to regulate their behavior.   N S U A NA

43. I reward subordinates for following rules and regulations. N S U A NA

44. I involve subordinates in developing orientation and induction programs for new staff. N S U A NA

45. I try to help each subordinate become self-directing. N S U A NA

8.0 Professional Development

46. I provide staff development programs for my subordinates. N S U A NA

47. I encourage my subordinates to develop specializations through staff development programs. N S U A NA

48. I work closely with my subordinates in developing staff development plans. N S U A NA

49. My staff development programs are based on the latest research findings. N S U A NA

50. Staff meetings in my unit are cooperatively planned with subordinates. N S U A NA

51. Demonstrations are frequently used in my staff development programs. N S U A NA

9.0 Extra-School Factors

52. I am as concerned about subordinates' personal problems as I am about their professional problems. N S U A NA

53. I counsel subordinates with respect to their personal problems. N S U A NA

54. I am aware of the personal problems confronting my subordinates. N S U A NA

55. I work with my superiors to provide counseling and/or referral services for employees. N S U A NA

56. I believe that helping subordinates solve or cope with their personal problems makes them better employees. N S U A NA

10.0 Conflict Management

57. I accept conflict as a normal part of all
    organizations.   N S U A NA

58. I manage conflict in a way that is beneficial
    to my organization.   N S U A NA

59. I serve as a mediator for interpersonal con-
    flicts within my unit.   N S U A NA

60. I call for external mediation when I cannot
    handle the conflicts in my unit.   N S U A NA

61. I assess the circumstances of each conflict
    before attempting to apply any conflict
    management techniques.   N S U A NA

Completing and Scoring the Inventory

The respondent should allocate approximately one hour for completing and scoring the inventory. Each item should be carefully read and responded to with complete honesty. The inventory should be viewed as a diagnostic tool that provides a rough indication of how well the leader facilitates morale in the work unit. By reviewing the scores in each section, the respondent can determine those areas where additional effort might improve morale.

Scoring the inventory is a simple process. Just complete the following table:

	Number	Weight	Weighted Score
Count the number of As:	_____ ×	4 =	_____
Count the number of Us:	_____ ×	3 =	_____
Count the number of Ss:	_____ ×	2 =	_____
Count the number of Ns:	_____ ×	1 =	_____
Total usable responses:	_____		

(Add number of As, Us, Ss, and Ns.)

Total weighted score   _____
(Add weighted scores for As, Us, Ss, and Ns.)

Divide total weighted score by total usable responses. This will give your overall score: _____

Interpreting Your Score

Your overall score will be between 1 and 4. A score of 1 is the lowest possible score and means that the leader's behaviors, attitudes, and skills tend to produce an *unfavorable* climate for subordinates' morale. A score of 4 is the highest possible score and means that the leader's behaviors, attitudes, and skills tend to produce a very *favorable* climate for subordinates' morale. Few leaders will score at the extreme positions on the scale. Most will score between 1.51 and 3.50, with the lower scores reflecting a tendency for the respondent to have a negative effect on morale, and the higher scores indicating a positive effect on morale.

Beyond getting the respondent's attention, the overall score is of little diagnostic value. Section and item scores are much more revealing and can serve a diagnostic purpose. Each section is scored in exactly the same way as the total instrument, except that only the items in the section are used in computing the section score. A worksheet is included in the Appendix for computing section scores.

To illustrate how the section scores may be interpreted, take the case of John Carter, whose section scores were as follows:

Overall	3.25
1.0 Leadership	2.21
2.0 Interpersonal Relationships	3.75
3.0 Rewards	3.62
4.0 Student Achievement	3.10
5.0 Workload	3.35
6.0 Facilities, Equipment, and Supplies	2.56
7.0 Control Mechanisms	3.29
8.0 Professional Development	1.78
9.0 Extra-School Factors	1.00
10.0 Conflict Management	3.76

John is doing well with interpersonal relationships (3.75), rewards (3.62), and conflict management (3.76). All indicate that his behaviors, attitudes, and skills in these areas have the potential of an extremely positive effect on his subordinates' morale. He should be pleased with these scores and continue to monitor his performance so that he does not regress in these areas.

John's behaviors, attitudes, and skills with respect to workload (3.35), student achievement (3.10), and control mechanisms (3.29) are satisfactory but could use some sprucing up. After treating some of the more serious problem areas, he may want to spend some time working on these areas.

The serious problem areas for John are leadership (2.21); professional development (1.78); extra-school factors (1.00); and facilities, equipment, and supplies (2.56). These are the areas in which John could improve. Where should he start?

We recommend that John first review each item in each of the four areas in which he has a low score. He should determine why he rated each item as he did and think about how he might improve in that area. Some of the problems have simple solutions, while others will require extended consideration and action. He should handle the simple ones quickly and initiate a plan to overcome the more complex difficulties. This approach will produce some immediate results, thus providing the motivation and momentum for tackling the more difficult problems.

Solving Difficult Morale Problems

The model of problem solving we recommend for the more difficult morale problems is one that has been around for a long time. Its steps are as follows:

1. Identify the problem.
2. Analyze why the problem is present.
3. Establish the result to be achieved.
4. Generate and assess alternative means of achieving the result.
5. Select the best alternative and implement it.
6. Assess whether the desired result was achieved.

This rational process of problem solving will work well for the more complex problems uncovered by the Inventory.

A specific example will clarify the use of the recommended approach. Assume that John scored low (1 or 2) on item six, "I involve my subordinates in setting or changing the mission, goals, and objectives of the unit." He begins to analyze the problem by asking why he scored himself so low. He determines that he has an authoritarian approach to leadership, that he must always assume the leadership role, and that he must be the initiator of any change in the direction of the unit. He has failed to realize that others have excellent ideas and that those ideas should be included in the dialogue on the mission of the unit. The result he wishes to accomplish is free, open participation of all members in the mission, goals, and objectives of the unit; he wants his staff to "buy into" the unit, to accept it as theirs, and to assume responsibility for its products as he has assumed such responsibility in the past.

John considers three alternatives for accomplishing the result: the staff meeting, individual contact and follow-up, and group representation. Since he is an elementary principal with a staff of 20 teachers, he decides that the staff meeting, involving all teachers, is the best way to go. If he had a larger staff, the formation of grade-level groups with elected representatives would have been a better approach. And, if he had a smaller number of teachers, individual contact and follow-up would have been feasible.

Thus John brings the teachers together in a meeting and places the problem before the group. A full discussion of his analysis and desired results is conducted. Teachers are not forced to participate in the activity, but they are asked to give it a try; and a schedule of meetings is arranged to discuss the mission, goals, and objectives of the school. John assumes the leadership in making the arrangements, chairing the group, encouraging discussion, analyzing group progress, and preparing summaries of the results of meetings. A final document of the mission, goals, and objectives is produced; and each staff member signs it, thereby indicating their participation in the preparation of the document and their acceptance of its contents. The document is not complete until each person has consented to the document or given reasons for not signing. Discussion and revision continue until a consensus is reached and all participants have signed. At no time should anyone be threatened into giving their consent. Such a procedure would negate the very purposes for which the activity was designed.

Once a consensus is reached, a final document is prepared and circulated to the staff for their use. The mission and goals document is included in handbooks and publicized to the school community. Reviews and alterations, using the same process as used in developing the original document, are made periodically.

Evaluation of the results should include a review of the document itself; the process used; the teachers' feelings about the school, the principal, and themselves; and any negative side-effects that may have occurred. If the document is useful and meaningful to the school community, if the process produced the "we" feelings and generated the desired ownership of the educational program, and if the number and timing of meetings did not negate the desired effects, John could rate his problem-solving venture a success and move to the solution of other problems. If it is not the success he expected, he should use the problem-solving process to solve the new problems that have arisen. In this way, the problem-solving model is cyclical and self-correcting.

6

Good Administrative Practice in a Nutshell

This chapter, in the form of a summary, provides 12 rules for all school leaders to follow in order to foster good morale. We state these rules directly in terms of do's and don'ts, without consideration of the mitigating circumstances discussed in preceding chapters, because we think they are the critical leadership behaviors associated with good morale.

Rule 1:   Be open and have good morale yourself.

Don't cut yourself off from teachers, community, and your superiors. Don't confine your communications only to written memos and formal meetings. If you think teachers are lazy, students are undisciplined, and superiors, parents, and teachers are out to get you, then these groups will surely live up to your expectations. If you yourself have poor morale, you are probably a victim of burnout or plain orneriness. Under such circumstances you should consider counseling, time off, or a new profession.

Rule 2:   Communicate at many levels.

Telling people what to do is not communication. Communication does not occur until *you* hear what *they* think they are saying, and *they* hear what *you* think you are saying. This does not occur automatically. Feedback and discussion are necessary to determine whether the message is understood and whether the receiver understands what is wanted. Communication should flow up, down, and laterally. The leader should establish a communication network so this happens.

Rule 3:   Involve others in setting objectives, planning, and decision making.

The best way to get understanding of what is wanted and willingness to do what is wanted is through involvement. Teachers need to be involved in setting objectives for staff development, planning curriculum, and making decisions about teaching methodology. Students need to be involved in decisions concerning conduct, dress, and school activities. Parents need to be involved in order to know what is expected of them and their children, as well as what the school can do for them. School boards need to be involved in decisions at the policy level on personnel practices and educational philosophy. All of these groups and others are part of the total system and, therefore, must be active participants in setting objectives and planning in those areas that affect them.

Rule 4:   Set planning priorities.

If you have set up good communication networks, you have the best information needed for setting planning priorities.

Rule 5:   Your job is to get things done, not to do them yourself.

Forget the admonition: To get a job done right, do it yourself. The more decisions you make yourself, the less time you will have for getting others involved in planning.

Rule 6:   Know the values and needs of your community, your students, and your staff.

This means you need to listen to a lot of people at their places of business — halls, classrooms, lounges, stores, offices, and clubs.

Rule 7:   Hold high expectations for staff, but recognize your responsibility to help them meet your expectations.

Administrators tend to spend too little time helping people learn how to do their jobs and to grow. As a result, many administrators end up complaining that they have to do everything themselves.

Rule 8:   Give recognition to those who are helping to advance the objectives of the school.

Recognition should be deliberate. Use it on both formal and informal occasions.

Rule 9:   Have written policy developed for procedures and regulations.

In addition to having written policies, they must be disseminated and publicized. However, this is not enough. Policy manuals tend to gather dust. Policy needs to be articulated and modeled in teacher meetings, student meetings, classrooms, hallways, PTA meetings, and conferences.

Rule 10: Exercise your authority.

Exercising authority involves vision and encouragement. Your authority includes deciding what is to be decided and by whom. It includes providing support, setting up communication networks, and enforcing policy.

Rule 11: Provide resources needed to achieve the school's objectives.

Resources include materials, time, clerical help, counseling, and staff development.

Rule 12: Do your best to obtain competitive salary levels so you can obtain the very best staff.

Good salaries enable one to compete in the marketplace for good people, those willing and able to provide a quality education for children and youth.

References

Allen, S.W. "The Administrative Use of Modeling as a Staff Development Technique." Doctoral dissertation, Virginia Polytechnic Institute and State University, 1984.

Aronson, E. "Private Conversation [with] a Missionary for Social Psychology." *Psychology Today* 18 (August 1984): 41-45.

Barnard, C.I. *The Functions of the Executive.* 30th anniversary ed. Cambridge, Mass.: Harvard University Press, 1966.

Bentley, R.R., and Rempel, A.M. *Manual for the Purdue Teacher Opinionaire.* 2nd rev. ed. West Lafayette, Ind.: Purdue Research Foundation, 1980.

Blau, P.M., and Scott, R. *Formal Organizations: A Comparative Approach.* San Francisco: Chandler Publishing, 1962.

Calhoun, F.S., and Protheroe, N.J. *Merit Pay Plans for Teachers: Status and Descriptions.* Arlington, Va.: Educational Research Service, 1983. (ERS Stock No. 219-21684)

Carpenter, H.T. "A Study of the Relationship of Merit Salary Schedules to the Morale of the Teaching Staff in Eleven Selected School Systems." Doctoral dissertation, New York University, 1959. *Dissertation Abstracts* 20 (1959): 4010-4011. (L.C. Card No. Mic. 60-1122)

Cedoline, A.J. *Job Burnout in Public Education: Symptoms, Causes and Survival Skills.* New York: Teachers College Press, 1982.

Chandler, B.J. "Salary Policies and Teacher Morale." *Educational Administration and Supervision* 45, no. 2 (1959): 107-10.

Chandler, B.J., and Petty, P.W. *Personnel Management in School Administration.* New York: World Book Company, 1955.

College Board. *Academic Preparation for College: What Students Need to Know and to Do.* New York: College Board Office of Academic Affairs, 1983.

Cuban, L. *The Urban School Superintendency: A Century and a Half of Change.* Fastback 77. Bloomington, Ind.: Phi Delta Kappa Educational Foundation, 1976.

Cullens, B. Unpublished report. Harrisonburg: Southeastern Illinois College, 1971.

Derr, C.B. "Conflict Resolution in Organizations: Views from the Field of Educational Administration." *Public Administration Review* 32, no. 5 (1972): 495-501.

Doolittle, R.J. *Orientations to Communication and Conflict: Modcom Modules in Speech Communications.* Chicago: Science Research Associates, 1976.

Drucker, P.E. *Management: Tasks, Responsibilities, Practices*. New York: Harper & Row, 1974.

Dubin, R. "Industrial Research and the Discipline of Sociology." In *Proceedings of the 11th Annual Meeting of the Industrial Relations Research Association*. Madison, Wisc., 1959.

Dubin, R. "Industrial Workers' Worlds: A Study of the 'Central Life Interests' of Industrial Workers." *Social Problems* 3, no. 3 (1955): 131-42.

Freudenberger, H.J. *Burnout*. New York: Bantam Books, 1980.

Gallup, G.H. "The 15th Annual Gallup Poll of the Public's Attitudes Toward the Public Schools." *Phi Delta Kappan* 65 (September 1983): 33-47.

Griffiths, D.E. *Administrative Theory*. New York: Appleton-Century-Crofts, 1959.

Herzberg, F. Personal letters to Loyd Andrew, January 1983.

Herzberg, F. *The Managerial Choice*. Homewood, Ill.: Dow Jones-Irwin, 1976.

Herzberg, F.; Mauser, B.; and Snyderman, B.B. *The Motivation to Work*. 2nd ed. New York: John Wiley & Sons, 1959.

Hirsch, L. "Max in Action: Pictures from a Dissertation." *National Elementary Principal* 62 (1983): 17-21, 52-54.

Hopkins-Layton, J.K. "The Relationships Between Student Achievement and the Characteristics of Perceived Leadership Behavior and Teacher Morale in Minority, Low Socio-Economic, and Urban Schools." Doctoral dissertation, University of Houston, 1980. *Dissertation Abstracts International* 41 (1981): 4910A-4911A. (University Microfilms No. 81-12334)

Hoppock, R. *Job Satisfaction*. 1935. Reprint. New York: Arno Press, 1977.

Hoy, W.K., and Appleberry, J.B. "Teacher Principal Relationships in 'Humanistic' and 'Custodial' Elementary Schools." *Journal of Experimental Education* 39 (1970): 27-31.

Hoy, W.K., and Miskel, C.G. *Educational Administration: Theory, Research, and Practice*. New York: Random House, 1978.

Katz, D., and Kahn, R.L. *The Social Psychology of Organizations*. New York: John Wiley & Sons, 1966.

Kerr, C. "What Became of the Independent Spirit." *Fortune* 48 (July 1953): 110-11.

Likert, R. *The Human Organization: Its Management and Value*. New York: McGraw-Hill, 1967.

Lortie, D.C. *School-Teacher: A Sociological Study*. Chicago: University of Chicago Press, 1975.

Maccoby, M. *The Gamesman*. New York: Simon & Schuster, 1976.

Maslach, C., and Pines, A. "The Burnout Syndrome in the Day Care Setting." *Child Care Quarterly* 6, no. 2 (1977): 100-13.

Mathis, C. "The Relationship Between Salary Policies and Teacher Morale." *Journal of Education Psychology* 50, no. 6 (1959): 275-79.

Mayo, E. *The Human Problems of an Industrial Civilization*. New York: Viking, 1960.

McCurdy, J. "Merit Pay: Complex Issue with Few Easy Answers." *Education USA*, 9 January 1984, pp. 137-52.

Miles, R.E. "Human Relations or Human Resources?" *Harvard Business Review* 4 (1965): 148-63.

National Commission on Excellence in Education. *A Nation At Risk: The Imperative for Educational Reform*. Washington, D.C.: U.S. Government Printing Office, 1983. (Doc. No. 065-000-001-77-2)

National Education Association. *Status of the American Public School Teacher, 1980-81*. Washington, D.C., 1982.

Nimmer, D.N. "Teacher Morale, Student Morale and Selected Teacher Characteristics." Doctoral dissertation, University of South Dakota, 1977. *Dissertation Abstracts International* 39 (1979): 5465A. (University Microfilms No.79-4928)

Parsons, T. *Structure and Process in Modern Societies.* Glencoe, Ill: Free Press, 1960.

Pascale, R.T., and Athos, A.G. *The Art of Japanese Management.* New York: Warner Communications, 1981.

Passarella, L.A. "The Relationship of Class Size to Teacher Morale and to Teachers' Perceptions of Their Own Educational Effectiveness." Doctoral dissertation, Rutgers University, 1977. *Dissertation Abstracts International* 38 (1978): 3817A. (University Microfilms No. 77-27954)

Peters, T., and Waterman, R. *In Search of Excellence: Lessons from America's Best-Run Companies.* New York: Harper & Row, 1982.

Phi Delta Kappa Commission on Discipline. *Handbook for Developing Schools with Good Discipline.* Bloomington, Ind.: Phi Delta Kappa, 1982.

Rahim, M.A. "Managing Conflict Through Effective Organization Design: An Experimental Study with the MAPS Design Technology." Doctoral dissertation, University of Pittsburgh, 1976. *Dissertation Abstracts International* 37 (1977): 4477A-4478A. (University Microfilms No. 76-30434)

Rist, M.C. "Our Nationwide Poll: Most Teachers Endorse the Merit Pay Concept." *American School Board Journal* 170, no. 9 (1983): 23-27.

Roach, D.E. "Dimensions of Employee Morale." *Personnel Psychology* 11, no. 3 (1958): 419-31.

Robinson, G.E. "Incentive Pay for Teachers: An Analysis of Approaches." *Concerns in Education* (May 1984). (Educational Research Service Stock No. 226-00003)

Sagness, R., and Gates, G. "Do Administrative Practices Make a Difference? A Study of Morale in Two Small Rural Intermountain West Communities." Unpublished manuscript, Idaho State University, 1983.

Schneider, B., and Lapido, B. "Feeling Good About Feeling Better: A Study of Teacher Morale in Two Suburban School Districts." Unpublished manuscript, Northwestern University, 1983.

Sergiovanni, T.J. "Factors Which Affect Satisfaction and Dissatisfaction of Teachers." *Journal of Educational Administration* 5, no. 1 (1967): 66-82.

Sergiovanni, T.J.; Burlingame, M.; Combs, F.D.; and Thurston, P.W. *Educational Governance and Administration.* Englewood Cliffs, N.J.: Prentice-Hall, 1980.

Simon, H. *Administrative Behavior.* New York: Free Press, Macmillan, 1976.

Smith, K.R. "A Proposed Model for the Investigation of Teacher Morale." *Journal of Educational Administration* 4 (1966): 143-48.

Sparks, G.M. "Synthesis of Research on Staff Development for Effective Teaching." *Educational Leadership* 41, no. 3 (November 1983): 65-72.

Stevenson, J. "Time to Stop Being Romantic About Education." Letter to the editor, *Brunswick* (N.C.) *Beacon,* 20 May 1982, p. 4.

Strauss, G. "Some Notes on Power Equalization." In *The Social Science of Organization,* edited by H.J. Leavitt. Englewood Cliffs, N.J.: Prentice-Hall, 1963.

Strickland, B.F. "A Study of Factors Affecting Teacher Morale in Selected Administrative Units of North Carolina." Doctoral dissertation, University of North Carolina at Chapel Hill, 1962. *Dissertation Abstracts* 23 (1963): 4598-4599. (University Microfilms No. 63-3526)

Suehr, J.H. "A Study of Morale in Education Utilizing Incomplete Sentences." *Journal of Educational Research* 56, no. 2 (1962): 75-81.

Tannenbaum, F. *A Philosophy of Labor.* New York: Alfred A. Knopf, 1951.

Tannenbaum, A.S.; Rosner, K.G.; Rosner, M.; Vianello, M.; and Wieser, G. *Hierarchy in Organizations: An International Comparison.* San Francisco: Jossey-Bass, 1974.

Taylor, F.W. *The Principles of Scientific Management.* New York: Harper and Brothers, 1914.

Thompson, J.D. *Organizations in Action*. New York: McGraw-Hill, 1967.

Twentieth Century Fund. *Making the Grade: Report of the Twentieth Century Fund Task Force on Federal Elementary and Secondary Education Policy*. New York, 1983.

Viteles, M.S. *Motivation and Morale in Industry*. New York: W.W. Norton, 1953.

Wagstaff, L.H. "The Relationship Between Administrative Systems and Interpersonal Needs of Teachers." Doctoral dissertation, University of Oklahoma, 1969.

Watson, G. "Five Factors in Morale." In *Civilian Morale*, edited by G. Watson. Boston: Houghton Mifflin, 1942.

Whyte, W.H., Jr. *The Organization Man*. Garden City, N.Y.: Doubleday Anchor, 1956.

Zaleznick, A. "Managers and Leaders: Are They Different?" *Harvard Business Review* 55, no. 3 (1977).

Appendix

Directions: To compute the score for each category in the Inventory, total the scores in each category and divide by the number of items rated.

Item

1.0 Leadership

  1 _____
  2 _____
  3 _____
  4 _____
  5 _____
  6 _____
  7 _____
  8 _____
  9 _____
    _____ Total   Leadership Score = _____

2.0 Interpersonal Relationships

  10 _____
  11 _____
  12 _____
  13 _____
  14 _____
  15 _____

16 _____

17 _____

18 _____

19 _____

_____ Total   Interpersonal Relationships Score = _____

3.0 Rewards

20 _____

21 _____

22 _____

23 _____

24 _____

25 _____

26 _____

27 _____

28 _____

_____ Total   Rewards Score = _____

4.0 Student Achievement

29 _____

30 _____

_____ Total   Student Achievement Score = _____

5.0 Workload

31 _____

32 _____

33 _____

34 _____

_____ Total   Workload Score = _____

6.0 Facilities, Equipment, and Supplies

35 _____

36 _____

37 _____

38 _____

39 _____

40 _____   Facilities, Equipment,

_____ Total   and Supplies Score = _____

7.0 Control Mechanisms

41 _____

42 _____

43 _____

44 _____

45 _____

_____ Total   Control Score = _____

8.0 Professional Development

46 _____

47 _____

48 _____

49 _____

50 _____

51 _____

_____ Total   Professional Development Score = _____

9.0 Extra-School Factors

52 _____

53 _____

54 _____

55 _____

56 _____

_____ Total   Extra-School Factors Score = _____

10.0 Conflict Management

57 _____

58 _____

59 _____

60 _____

61 _____

_____ Total   Conflict Management Score = _____